Pattern Insanity 2

50 More Detailed Patterns for Adults to Color

JACQUELINE WISNIEWSKI

© 2018 Jacqueline Wisniewski

Thank you for purchasing Pattern Insanity 2!

For best results I suggest tearing out the page you want to color and coloring it separately from the rest of the book. If you bend the spine backwards in multiple spots it should open more flatly, making it easier to tear out each page cleanly.

Please note:
- All images are one-sided for the best coloring experience.
- The publisher only offered one kind of paper weight, so I strongly suggest <u>not</u> using alcohol-based markers in this coloring book, as they will bleed through significantly. However, other types of markers, gel pens, and colored pencils will work wonderfully.

Grab your favorite supplies, get comfortable, and enjoy the experience of coloring Pattern Insanity 2.

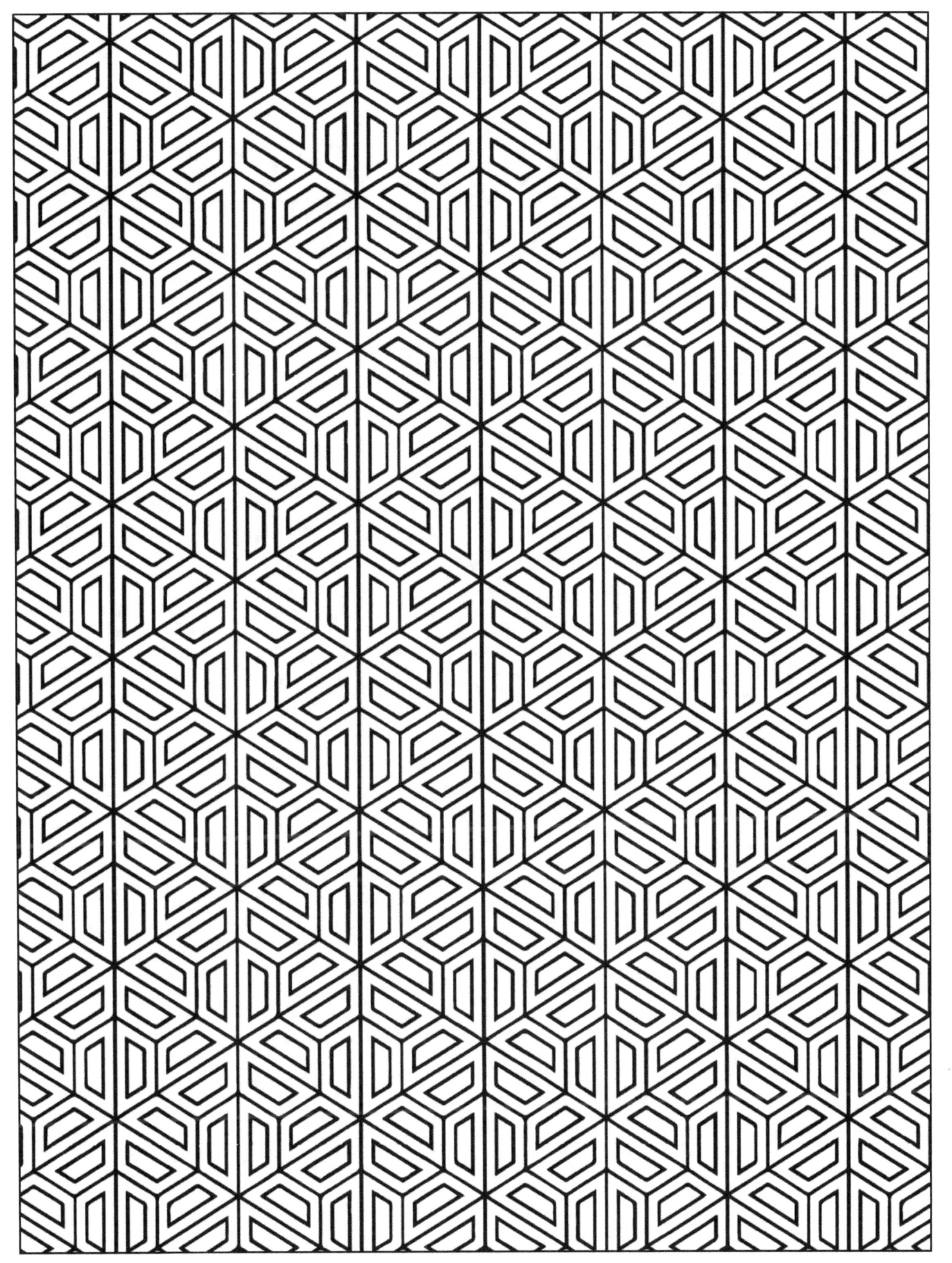

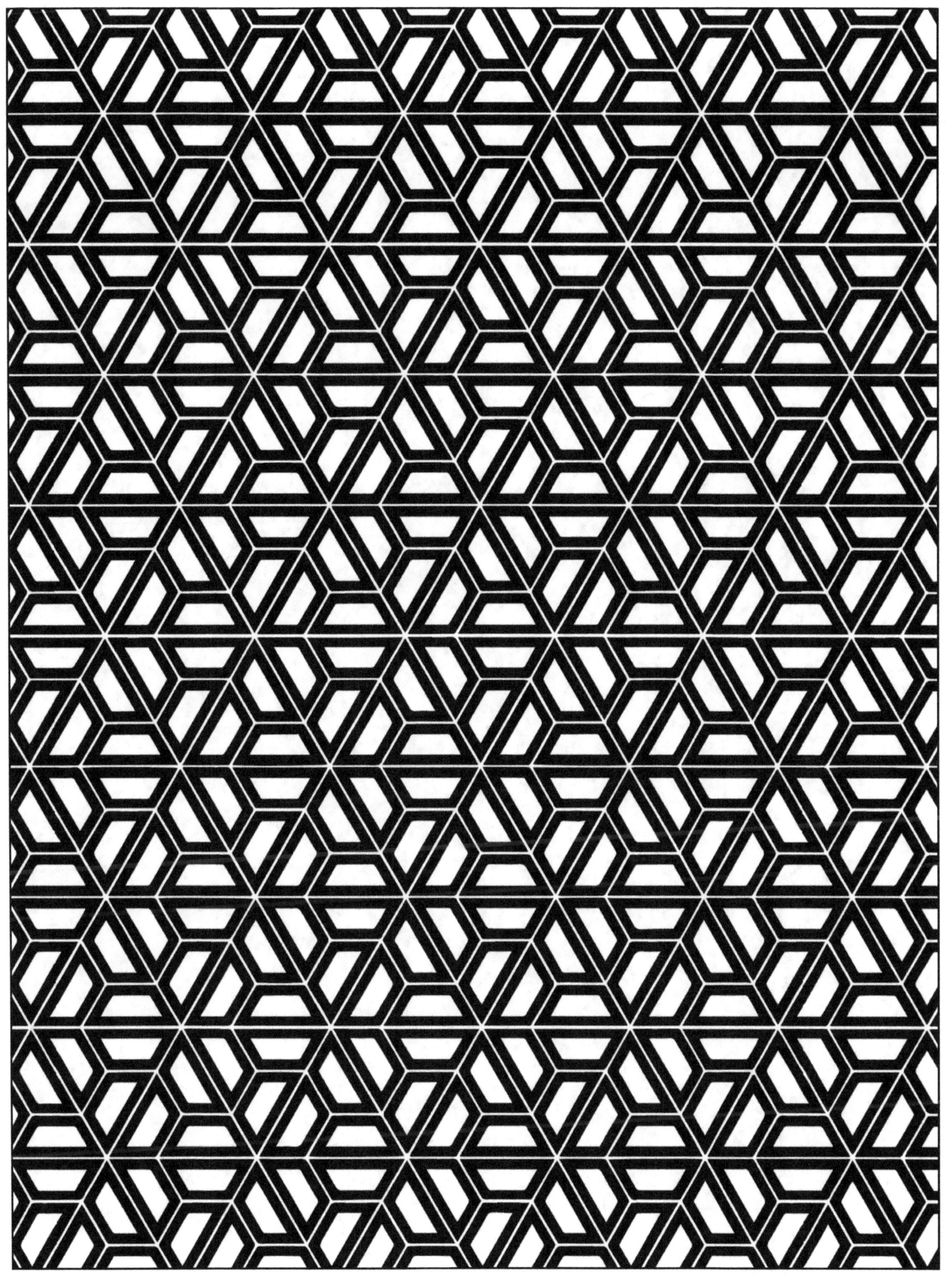

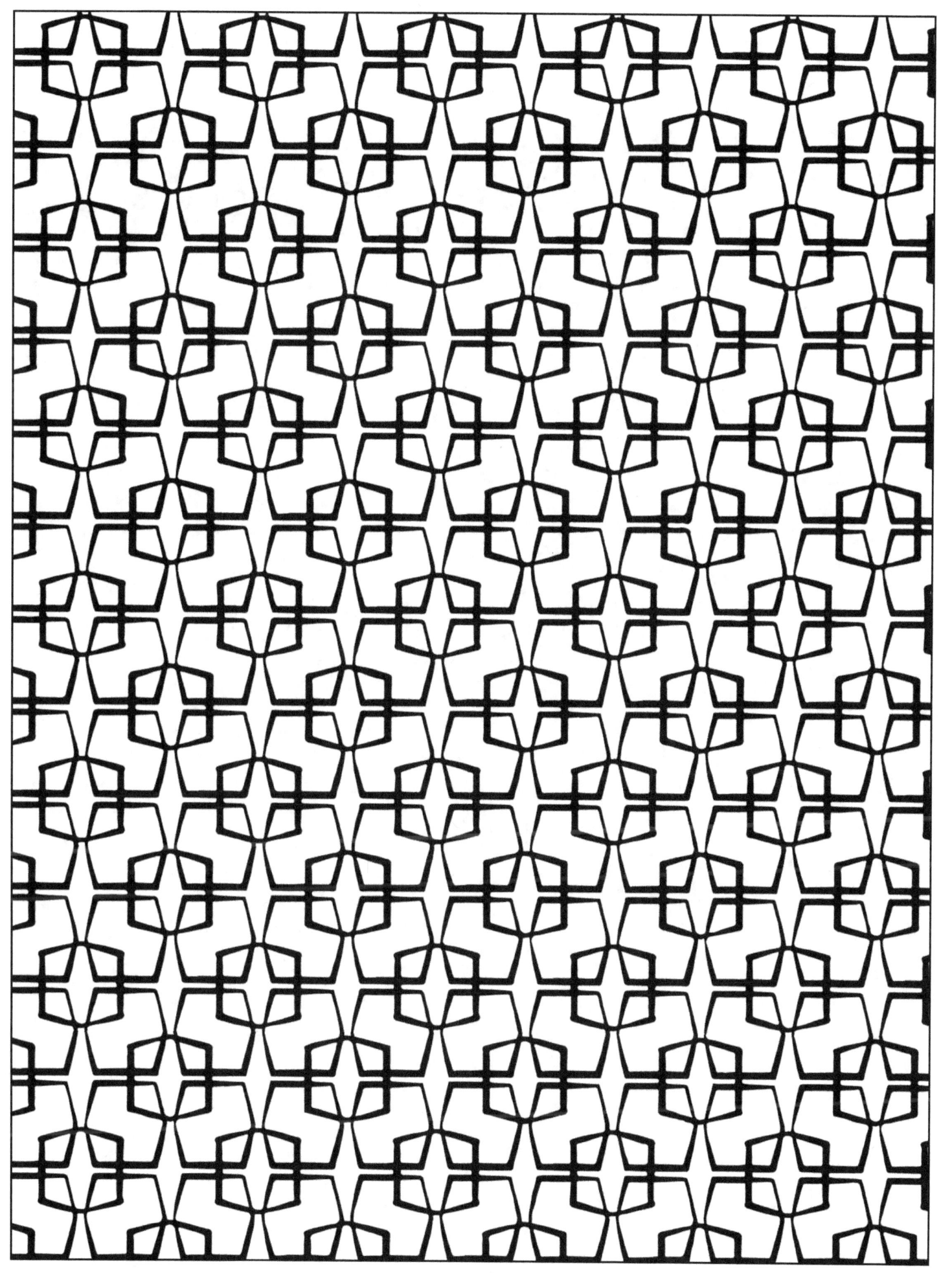

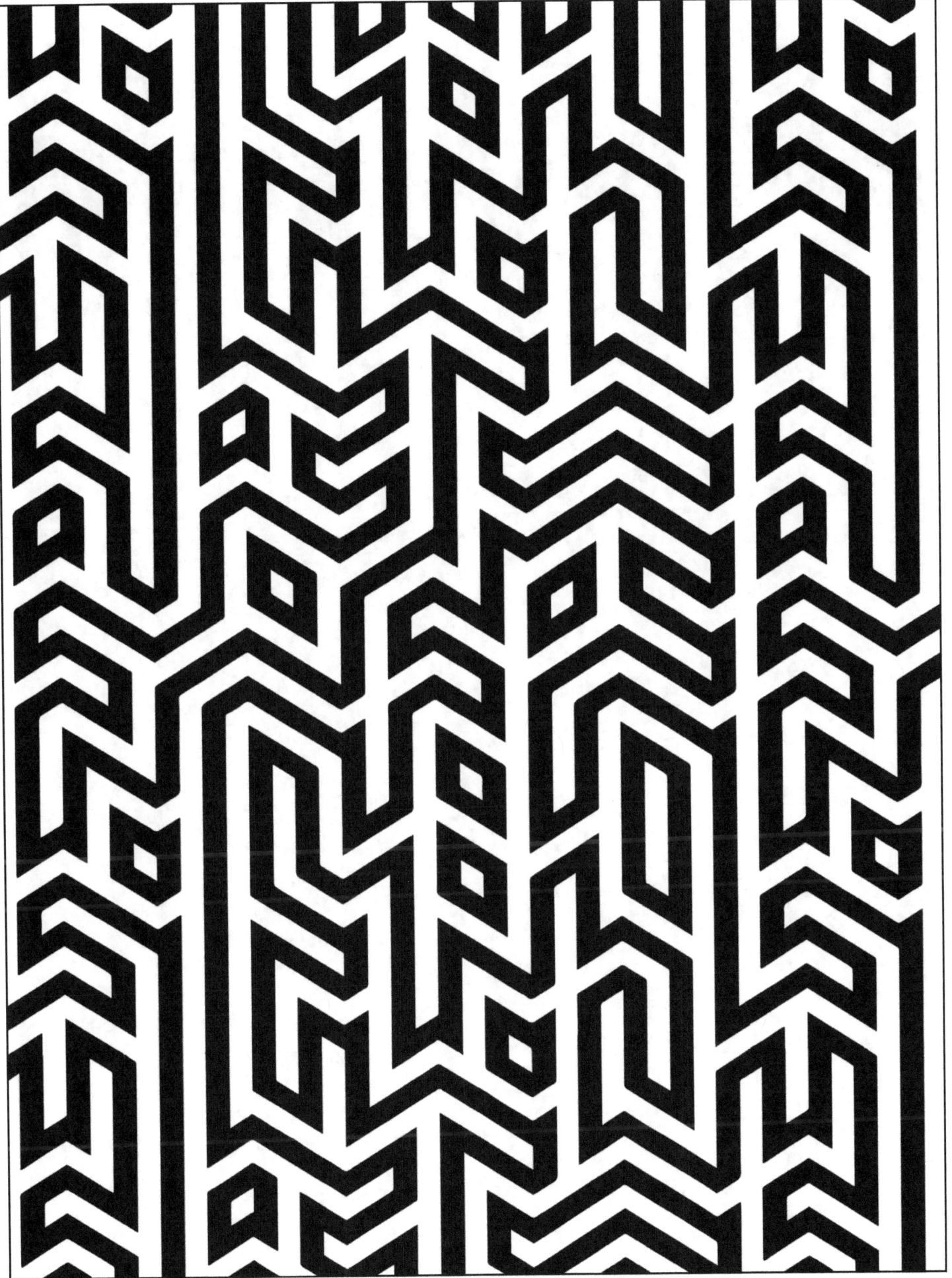

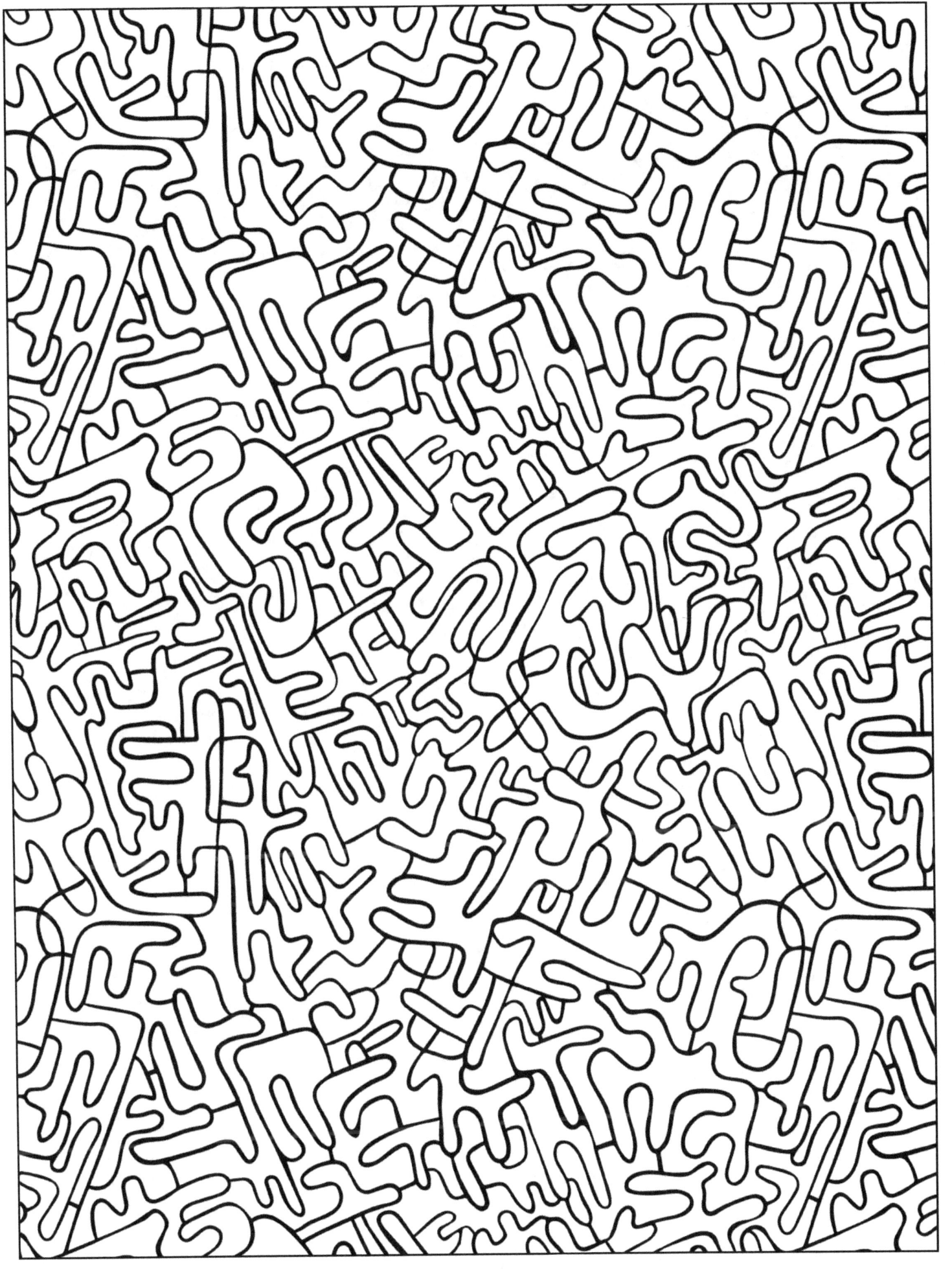

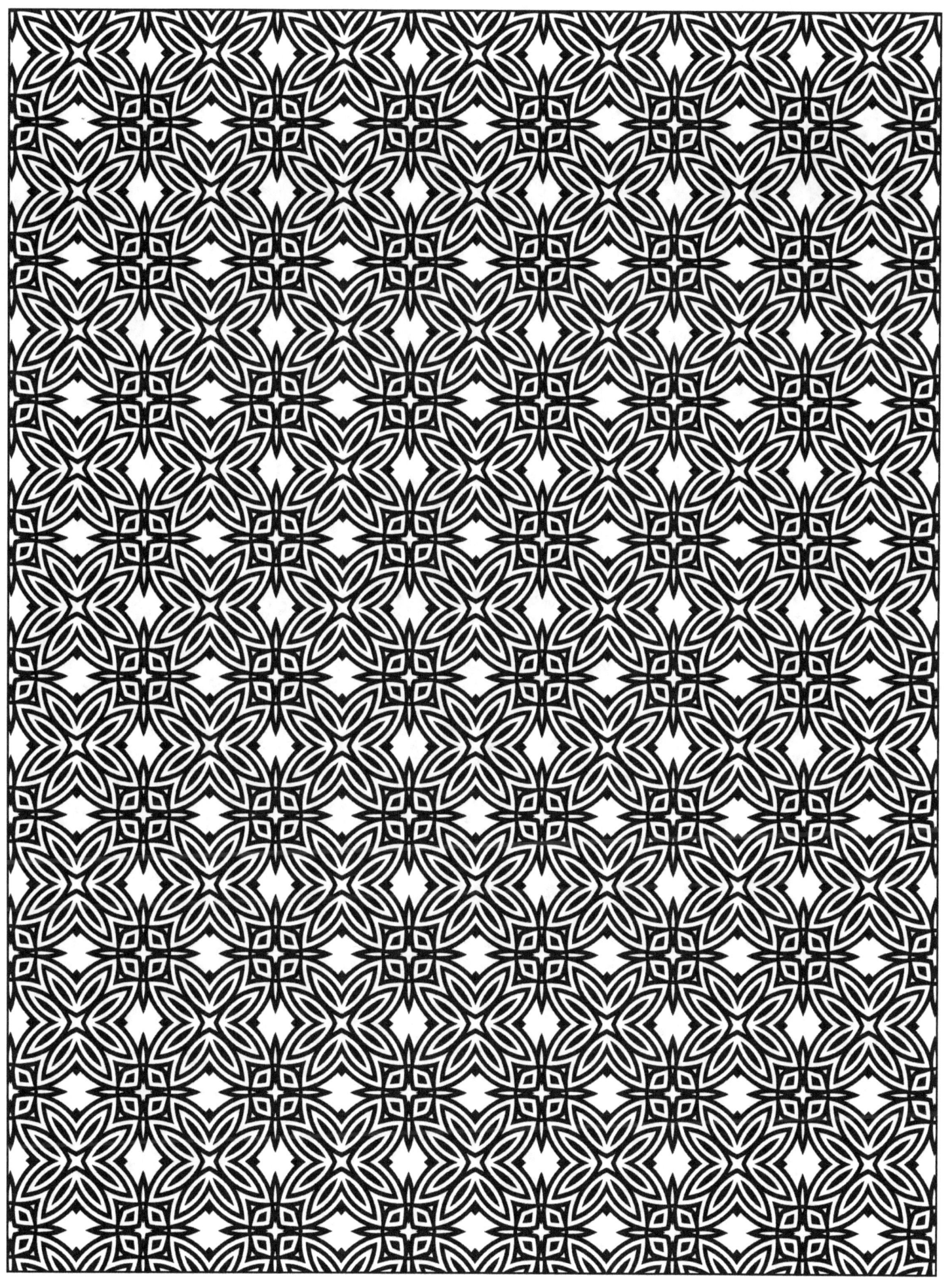

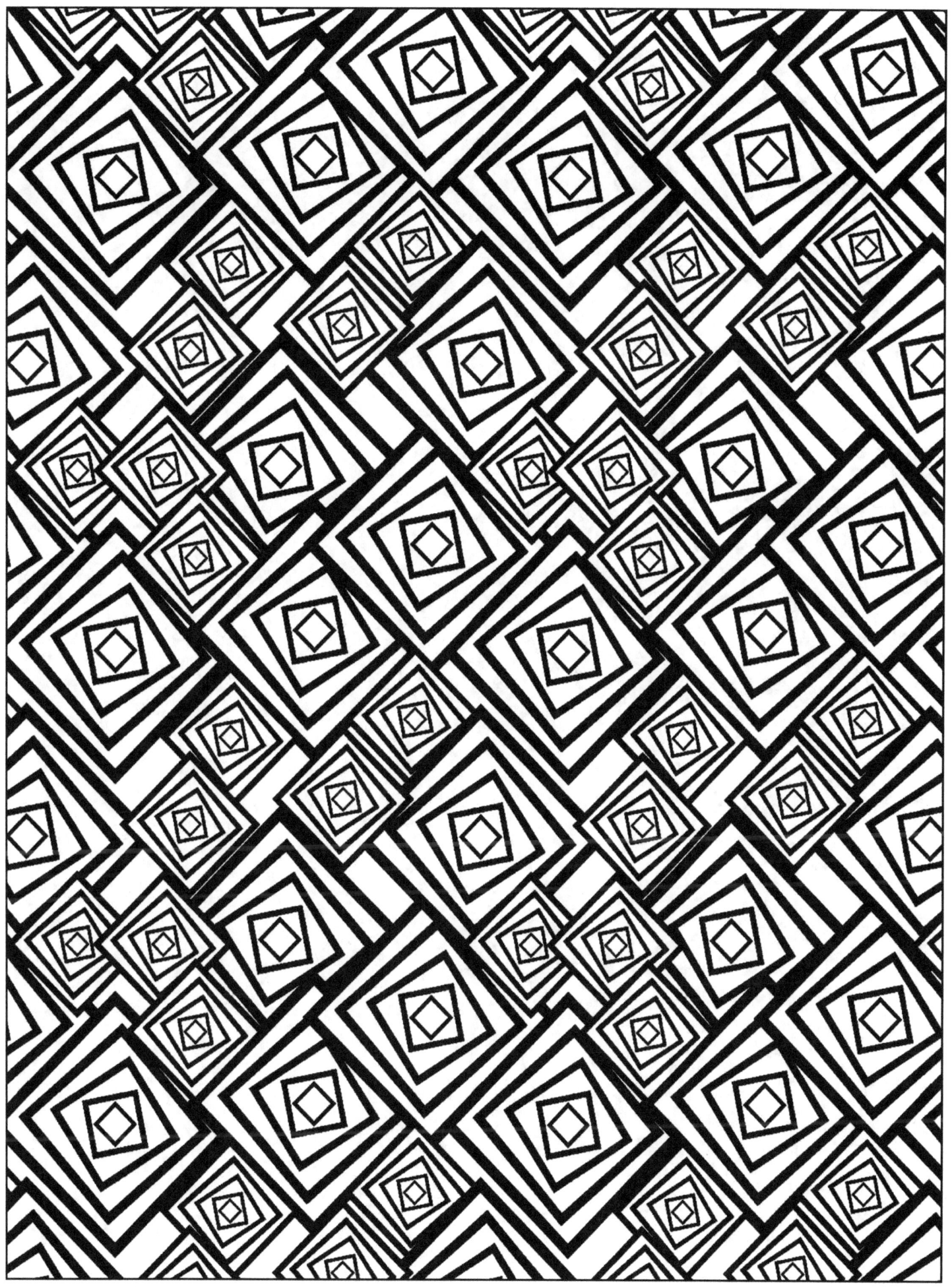

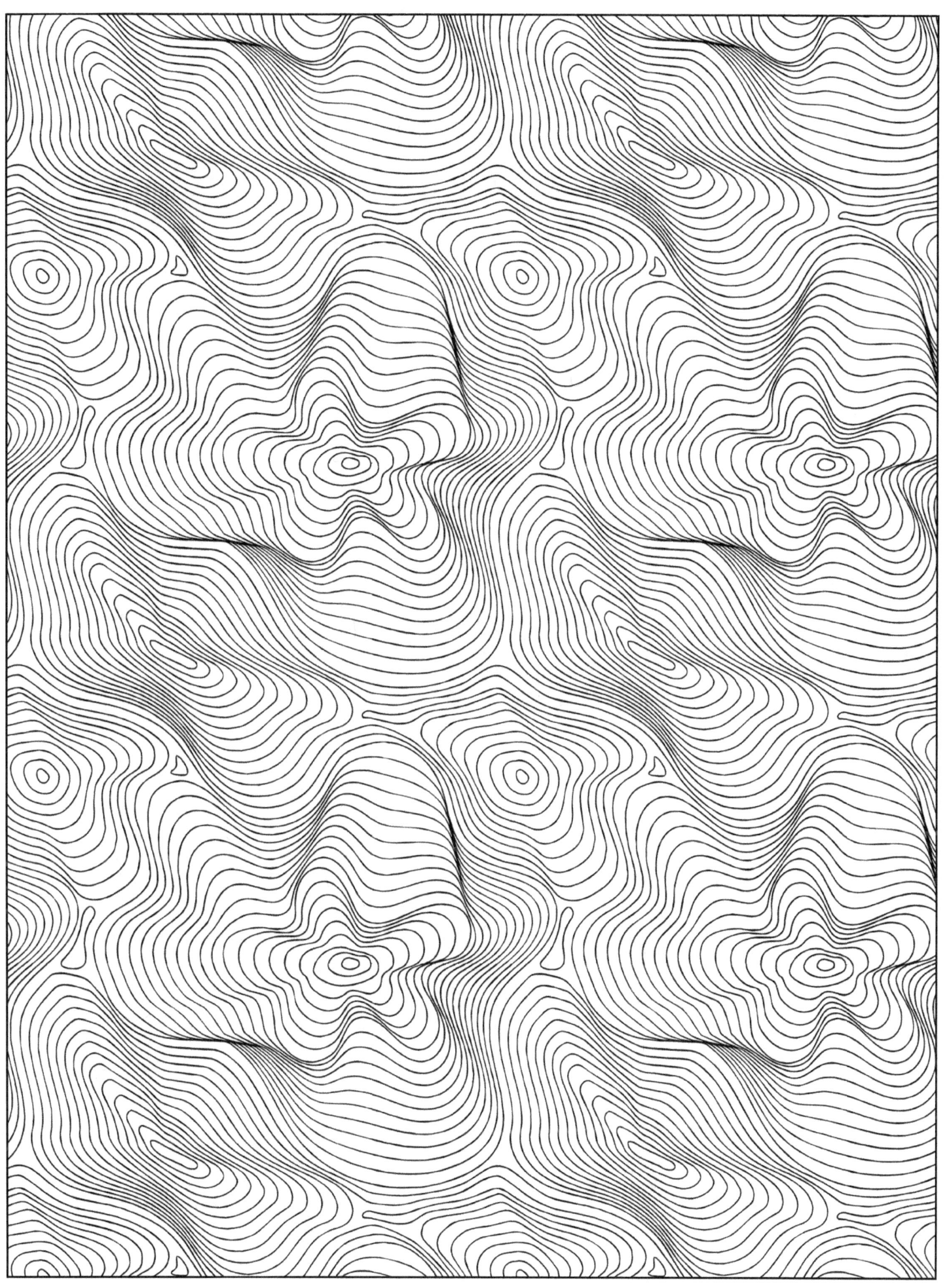

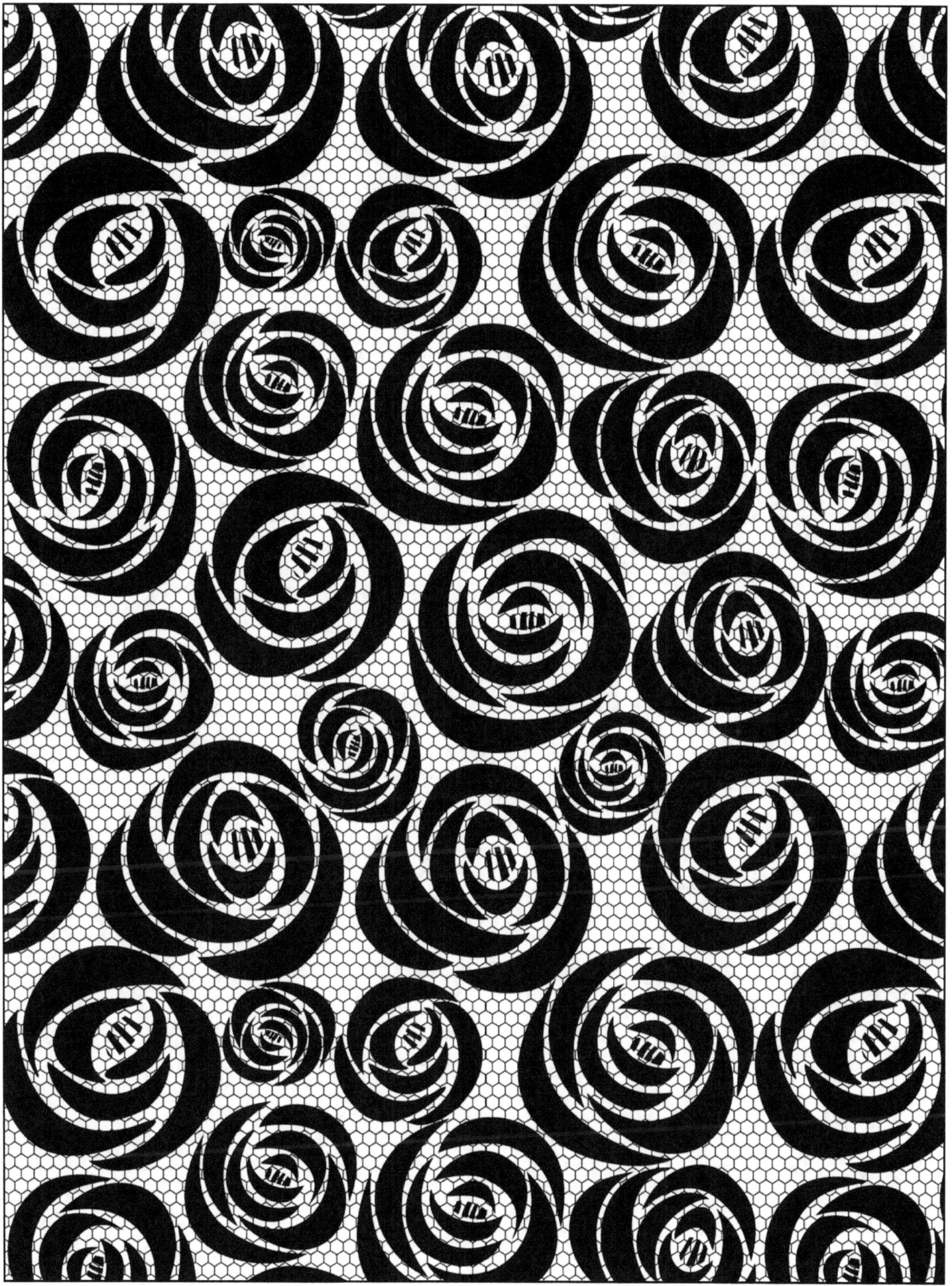

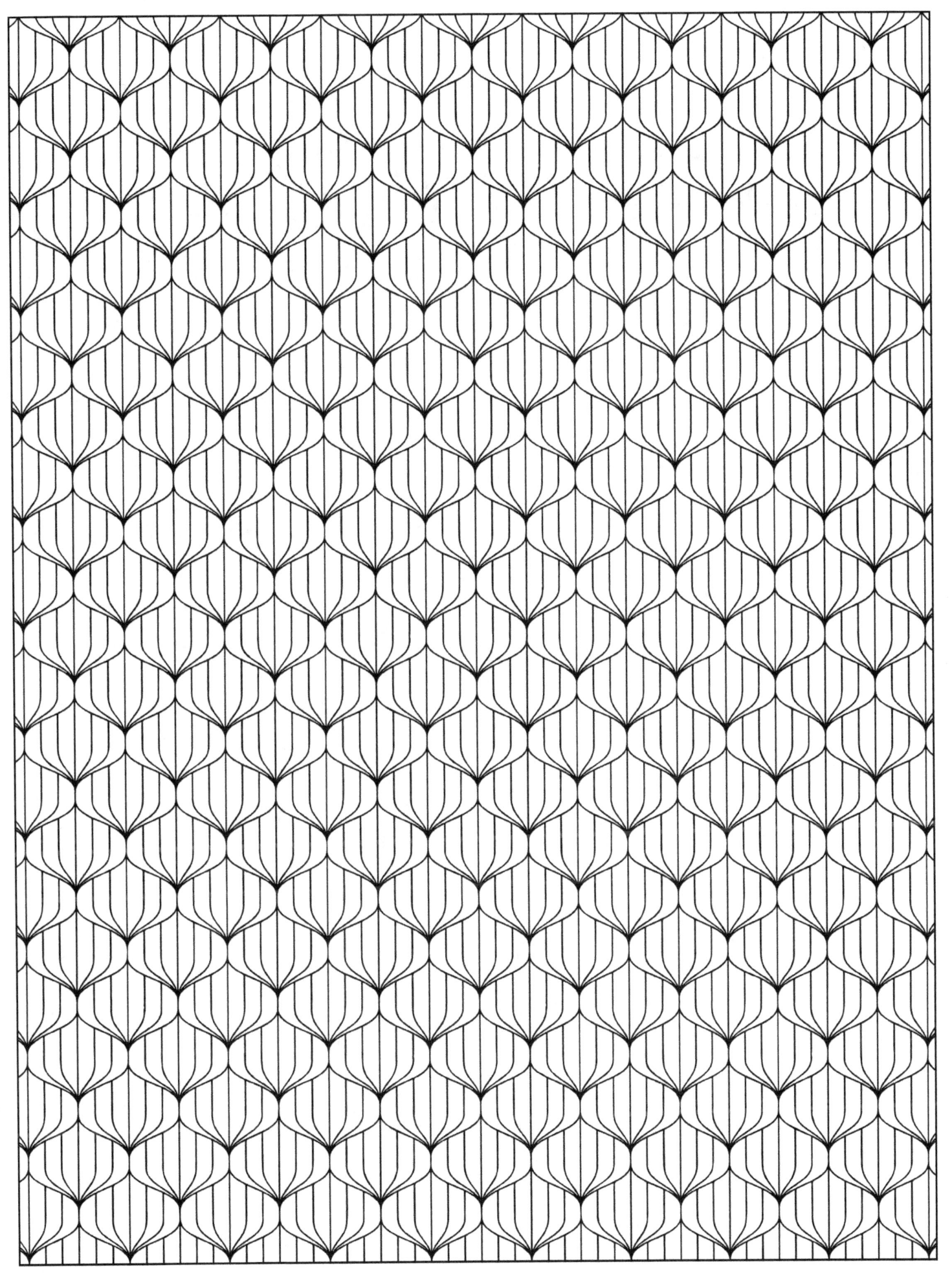

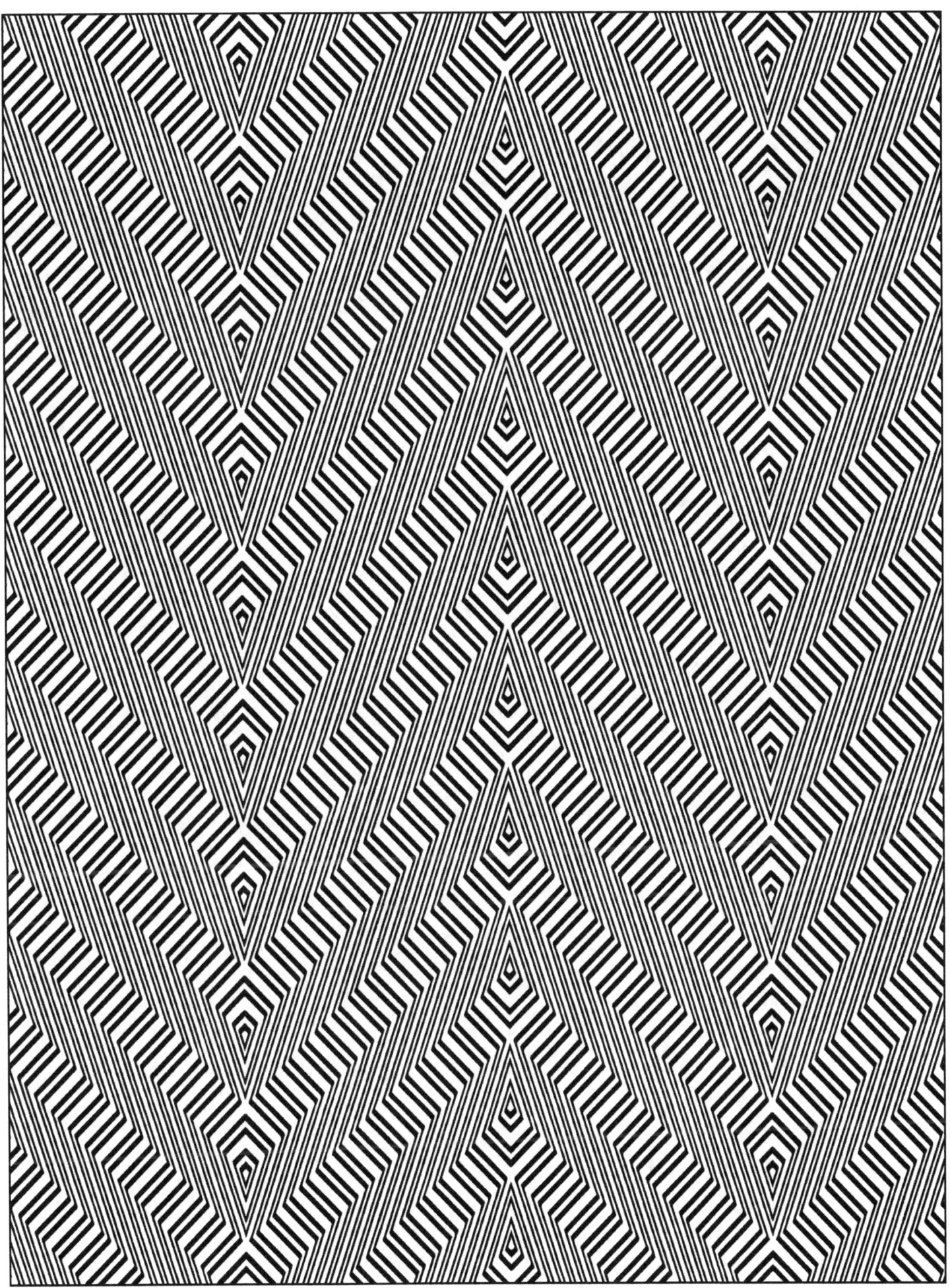

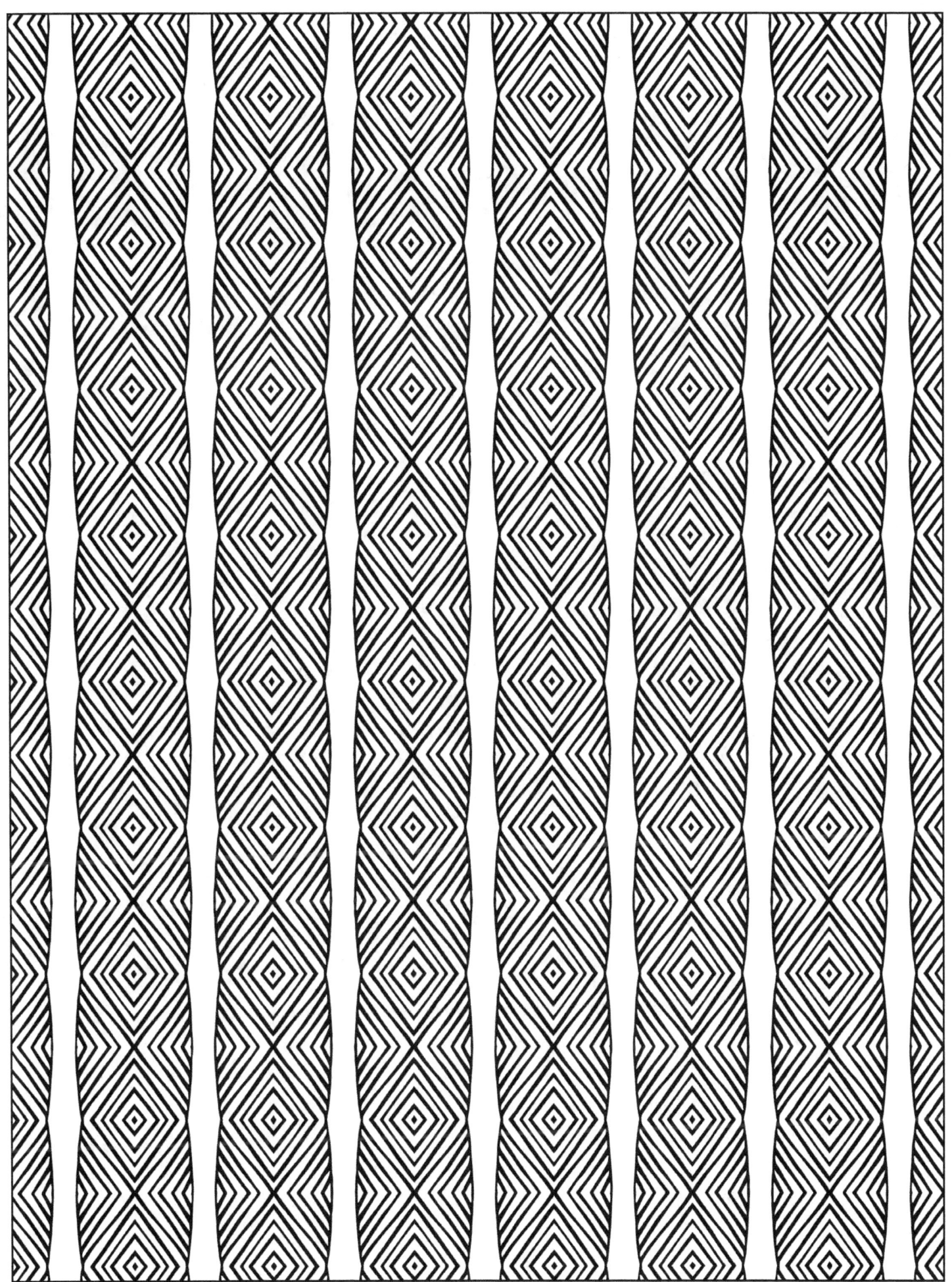

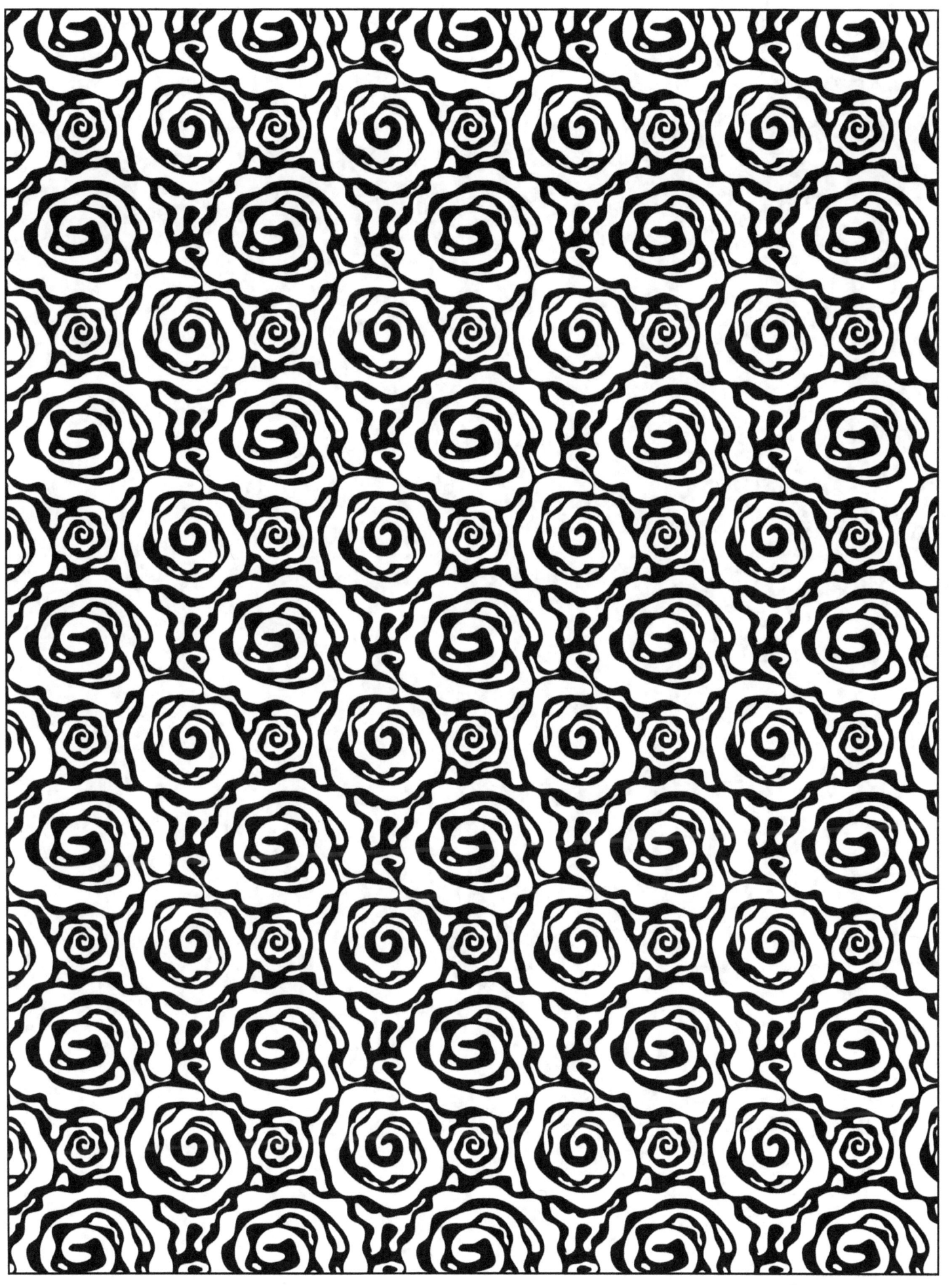

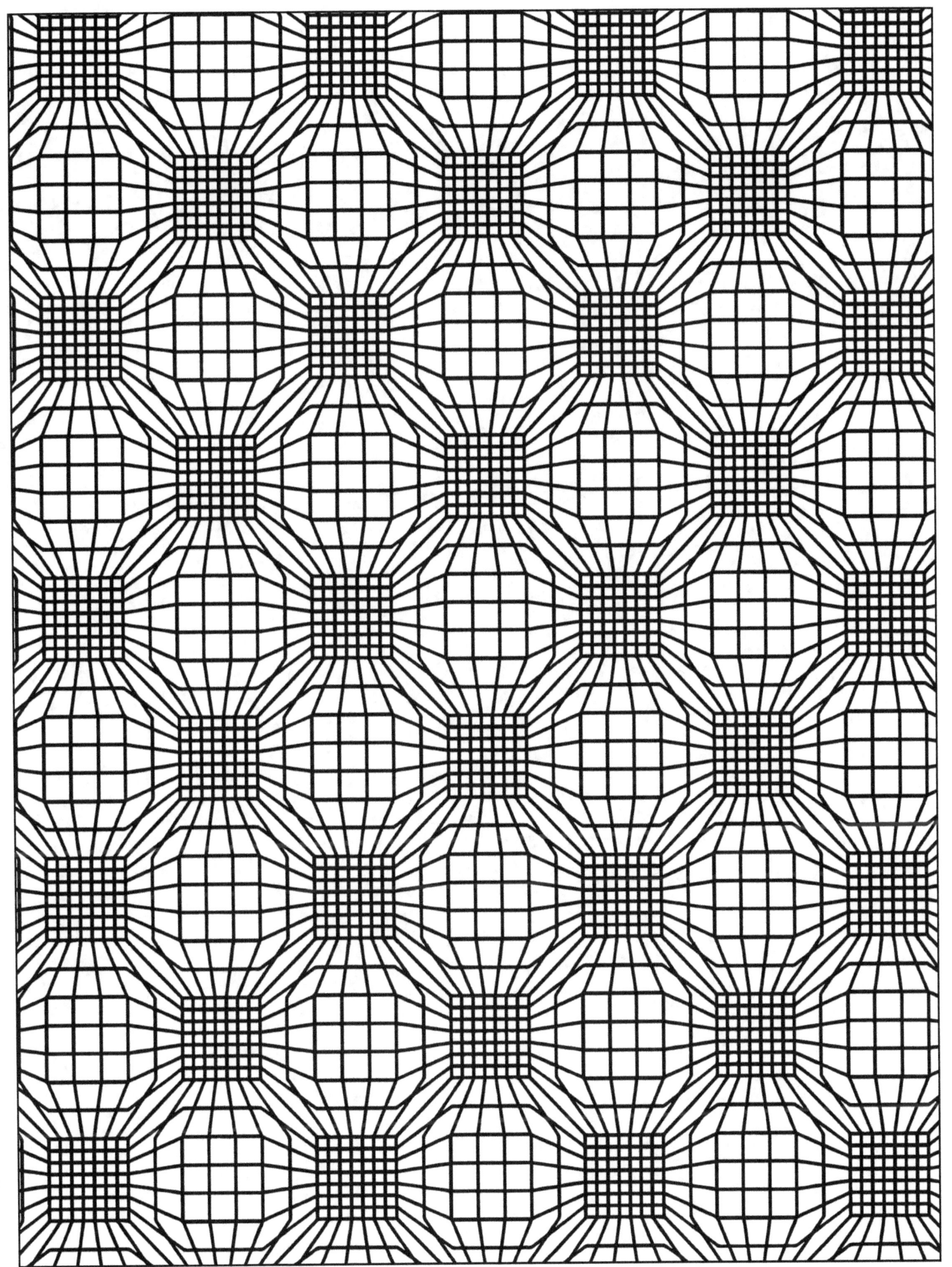

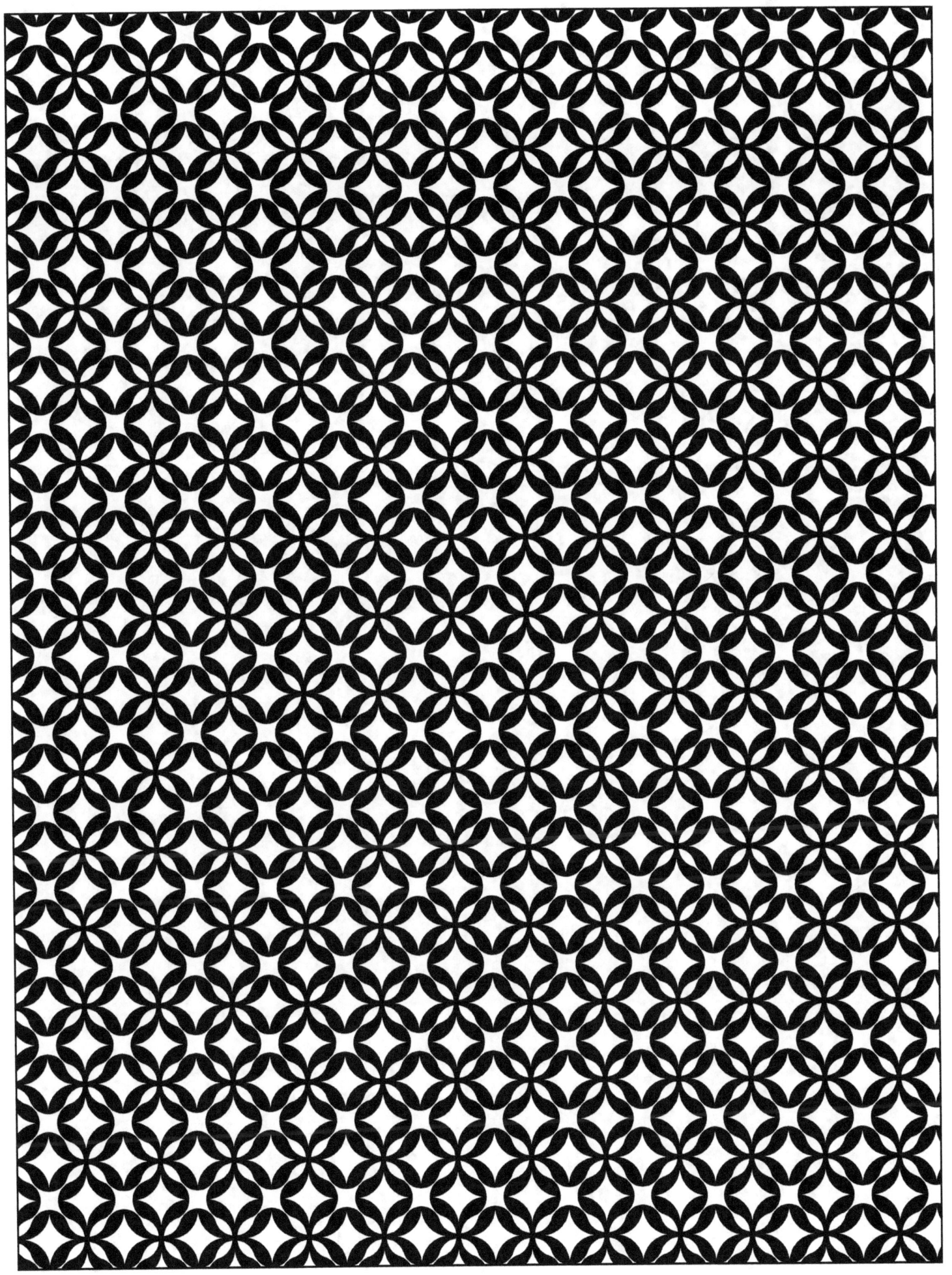

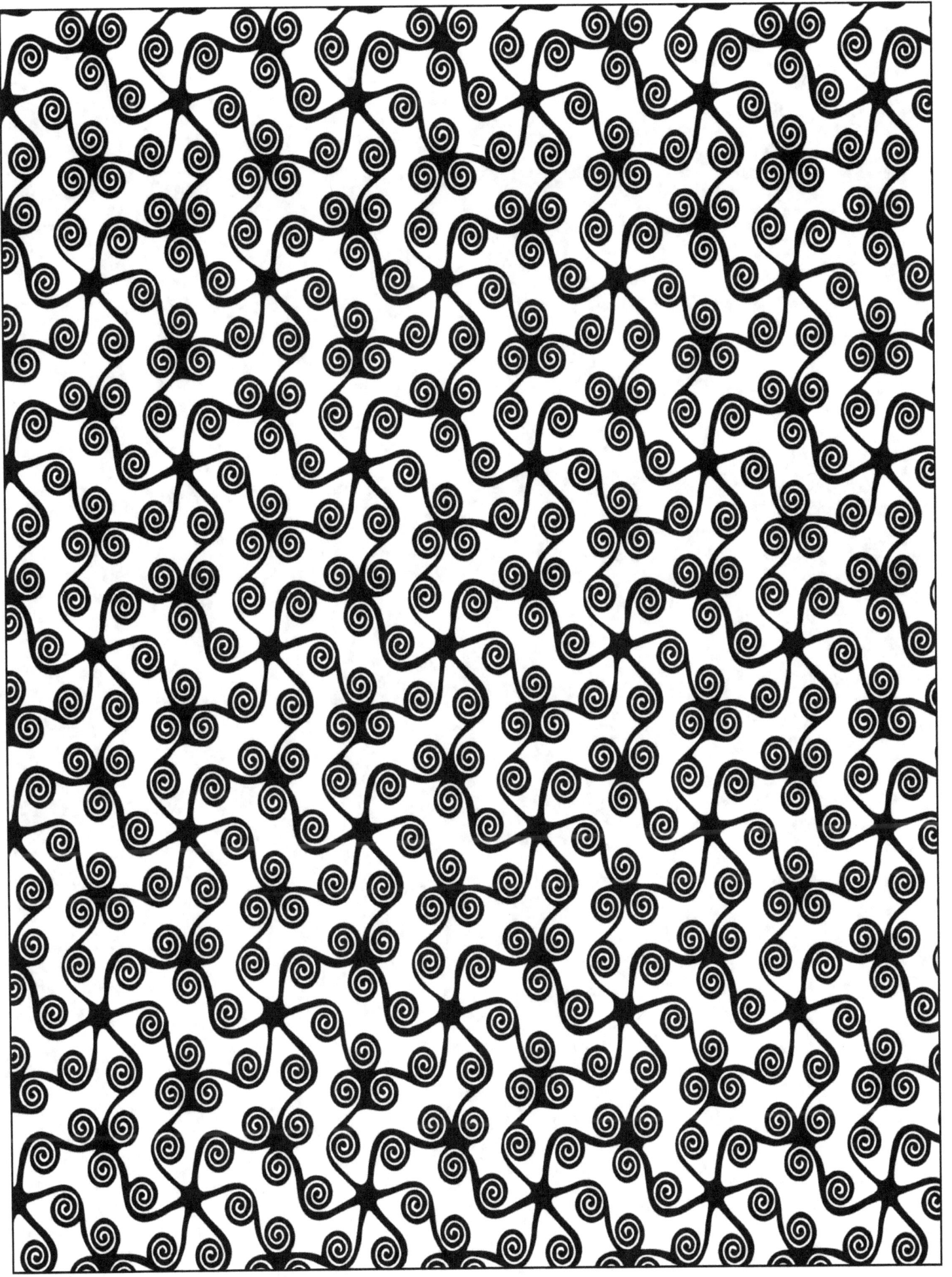

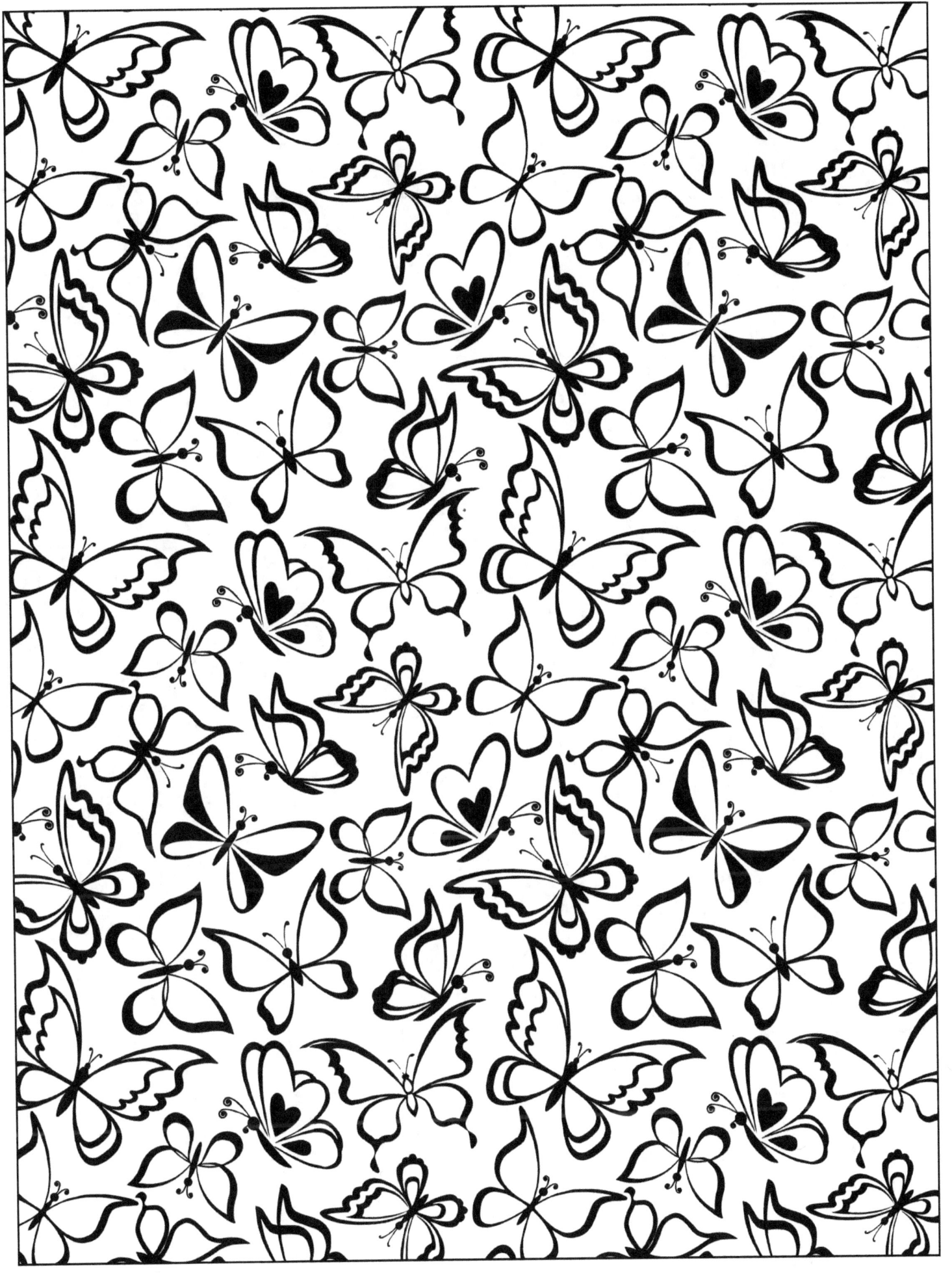

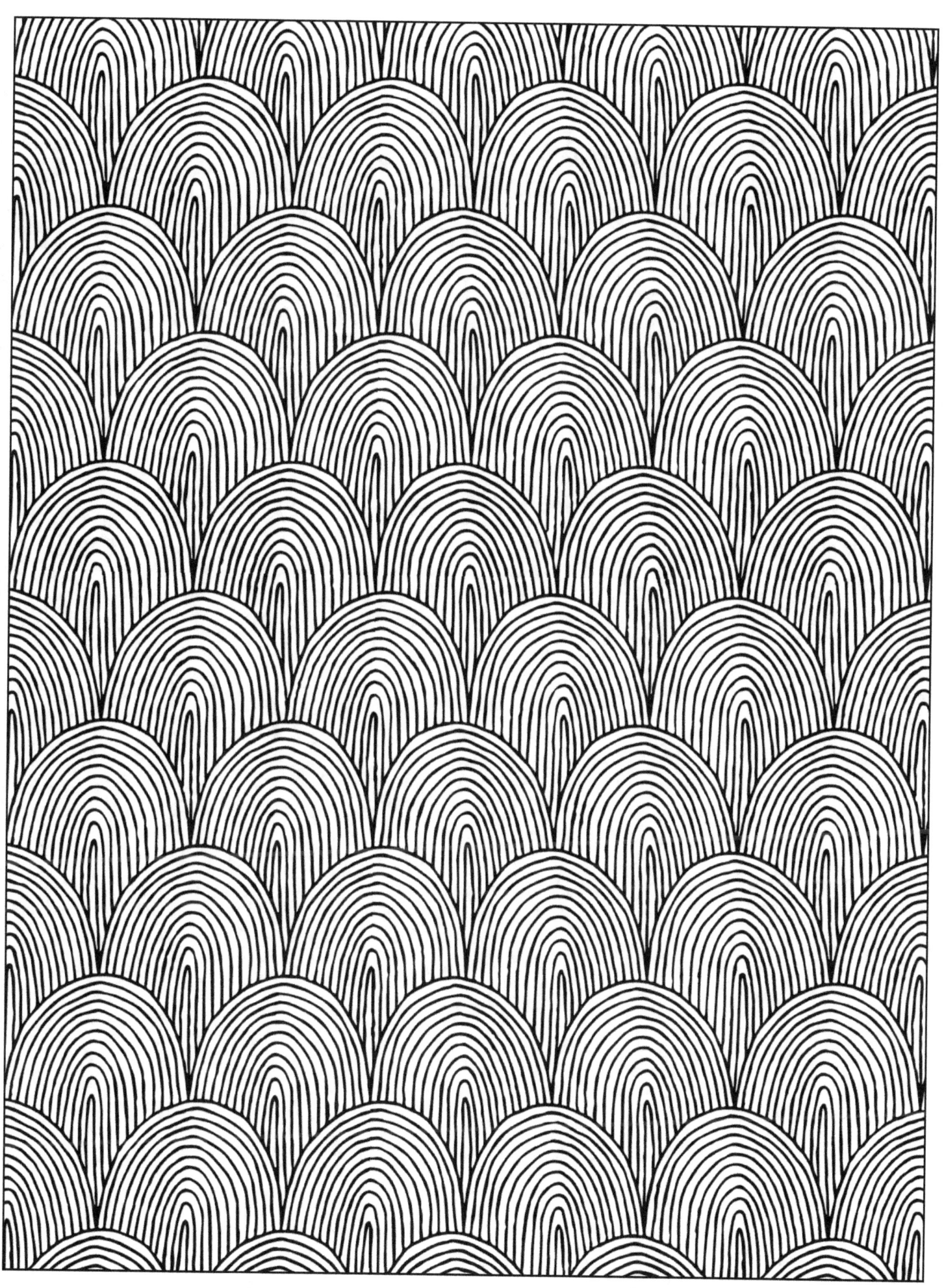

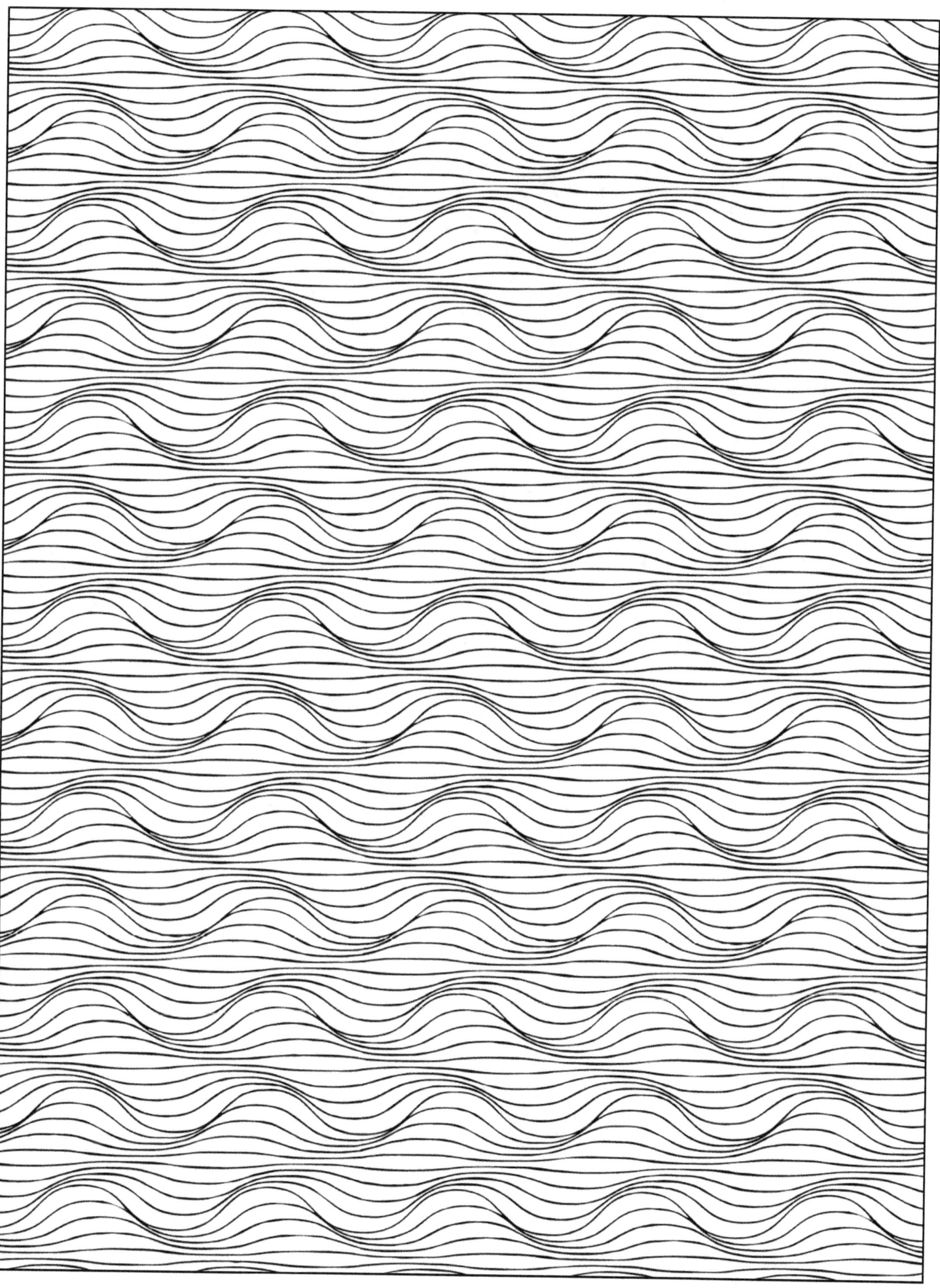

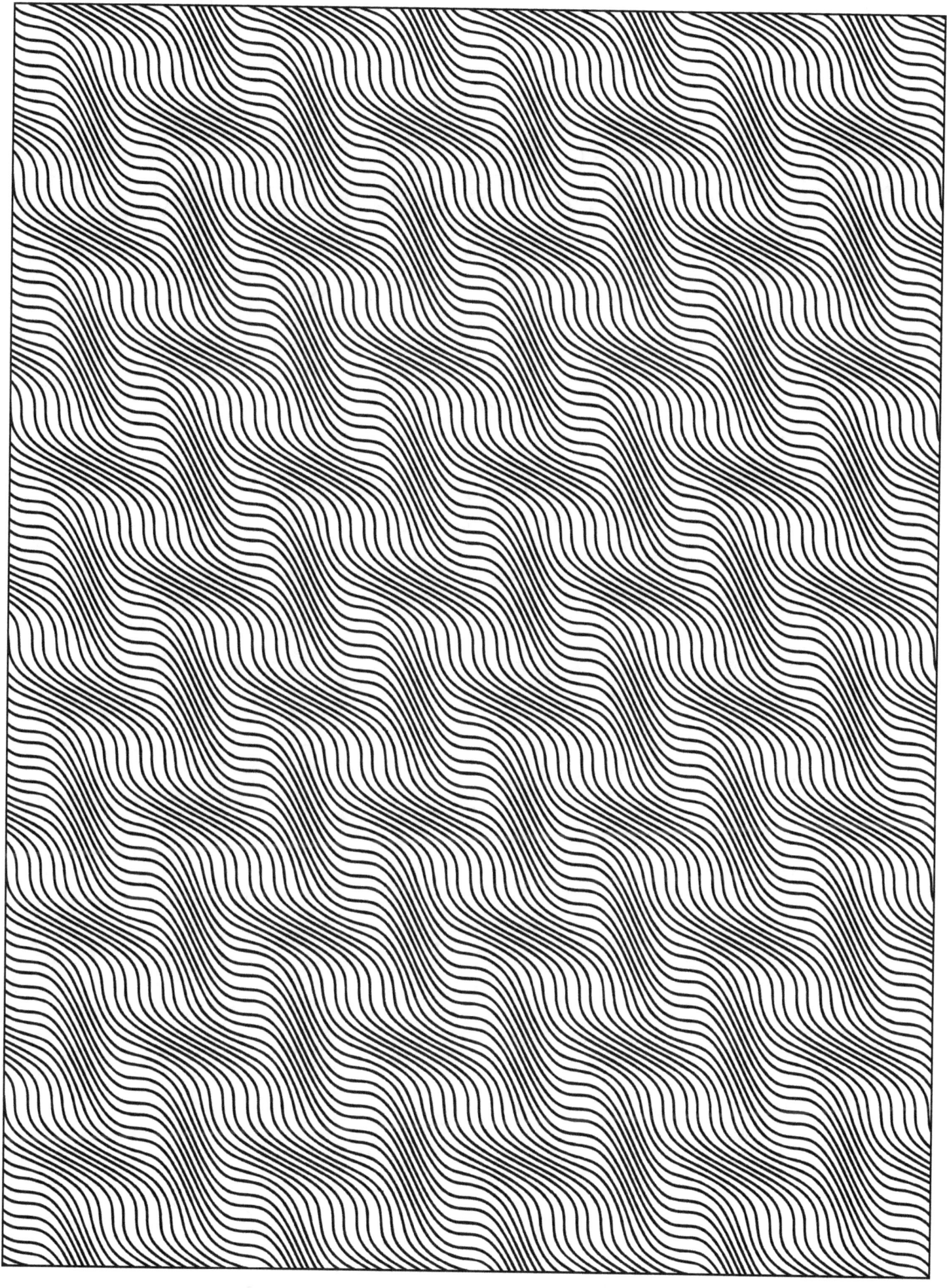

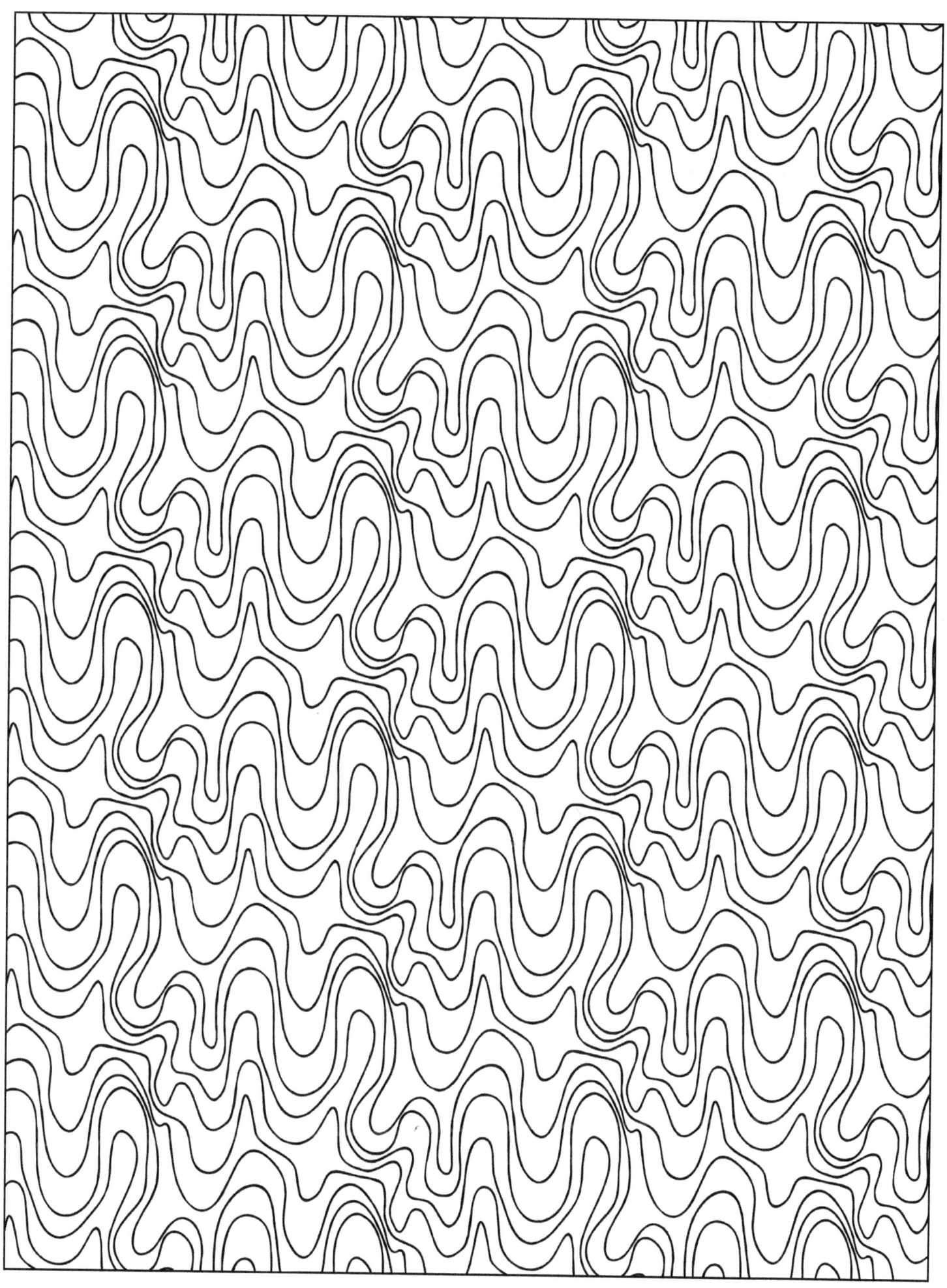

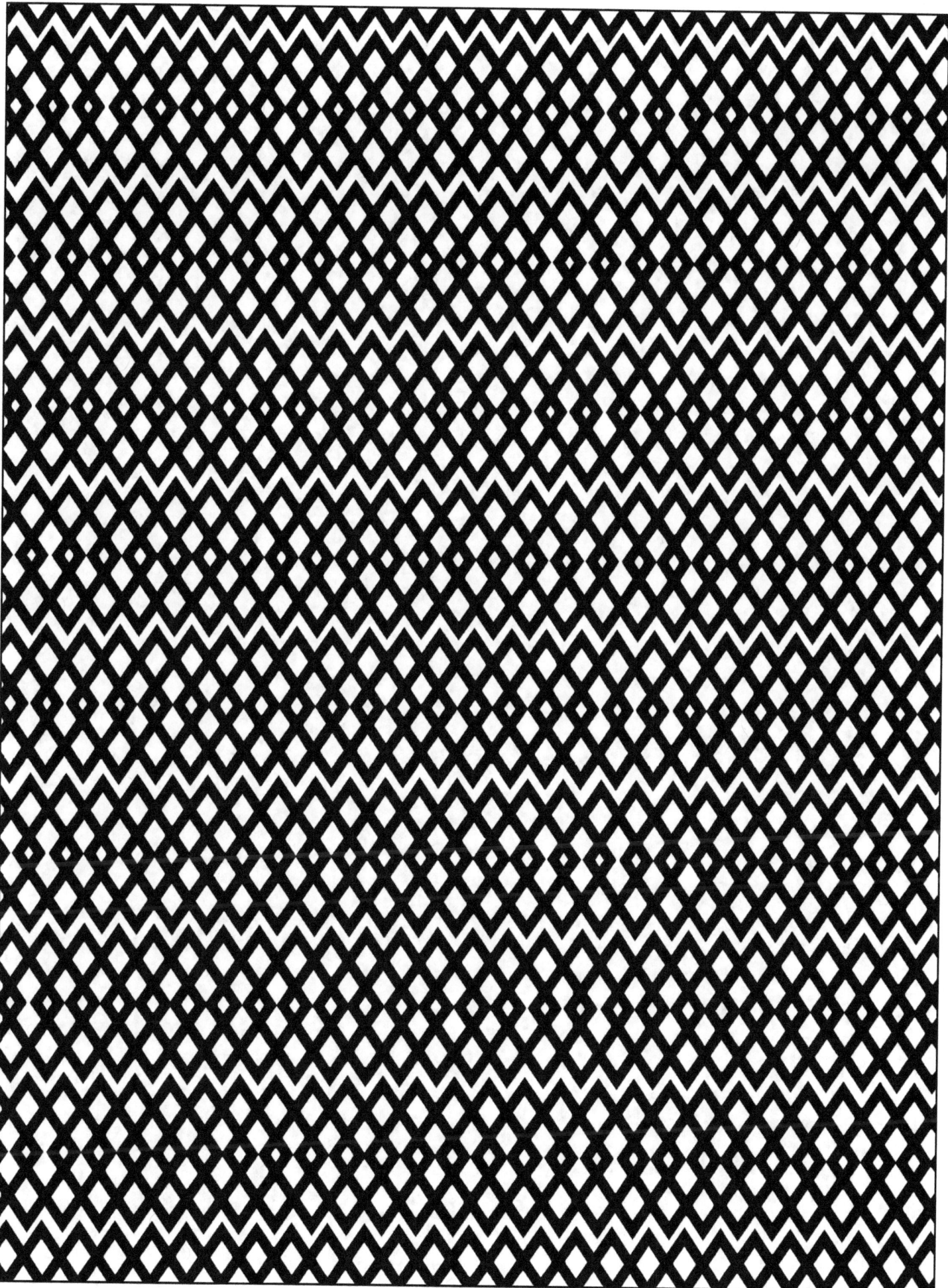

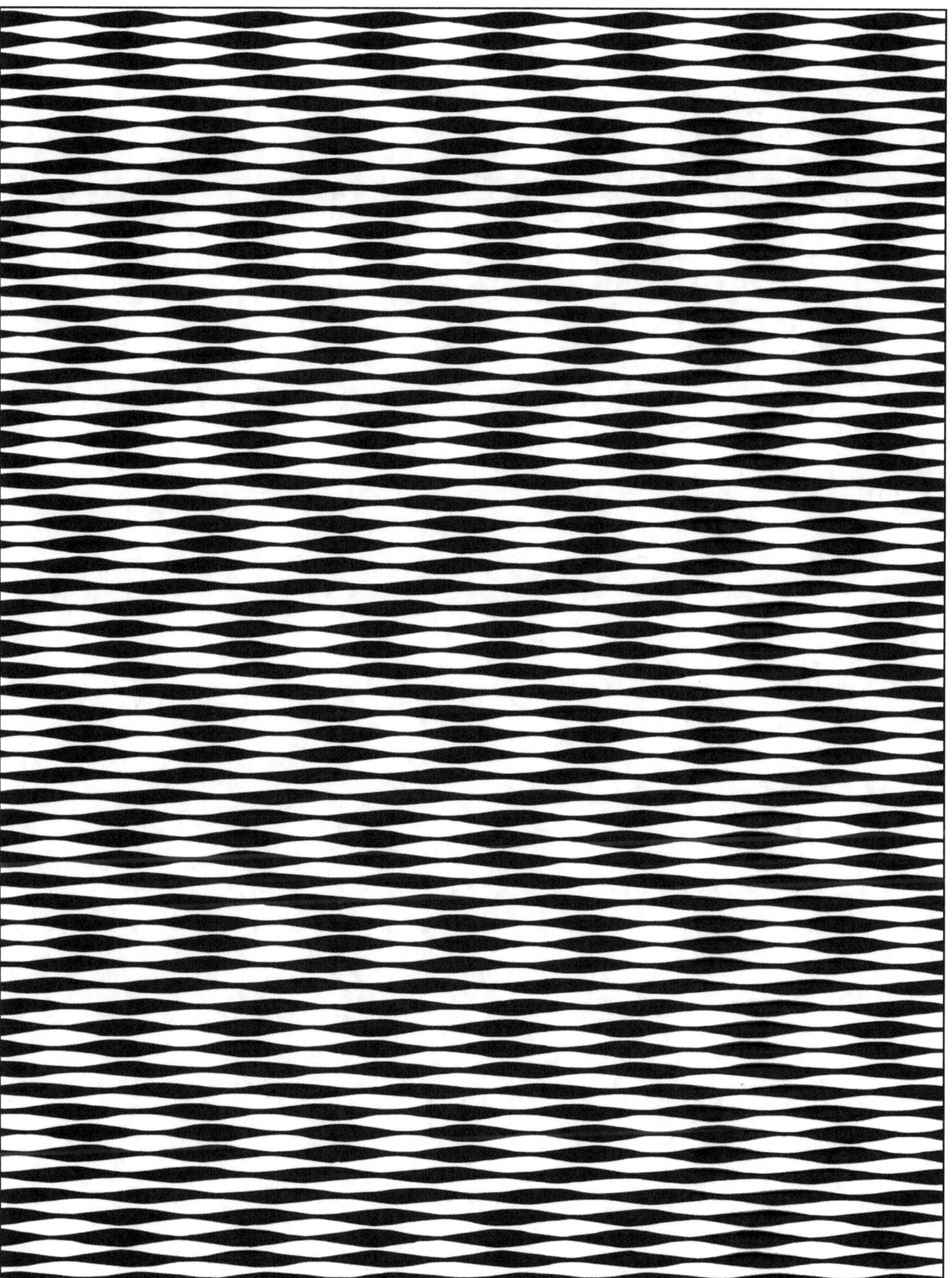

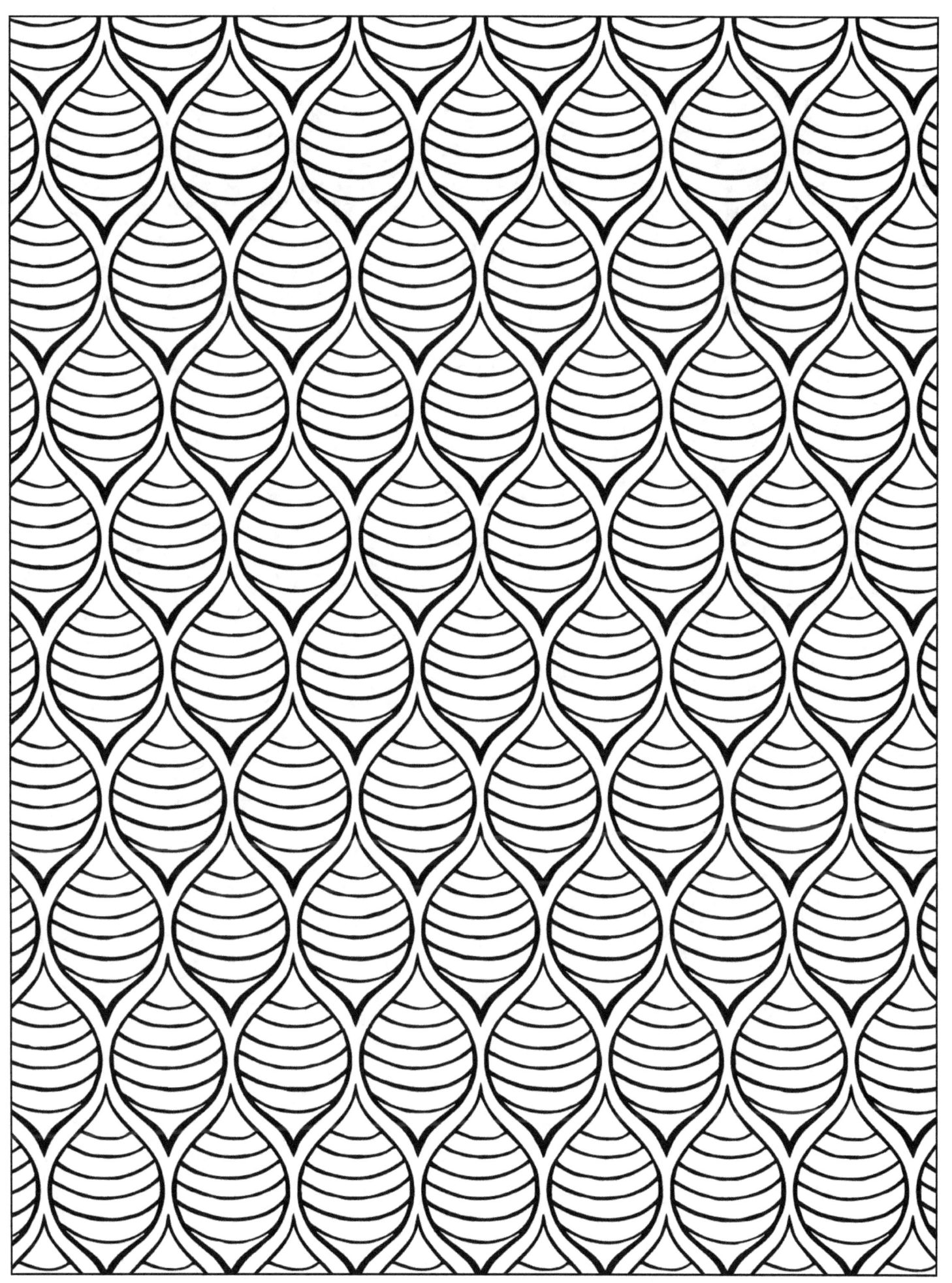

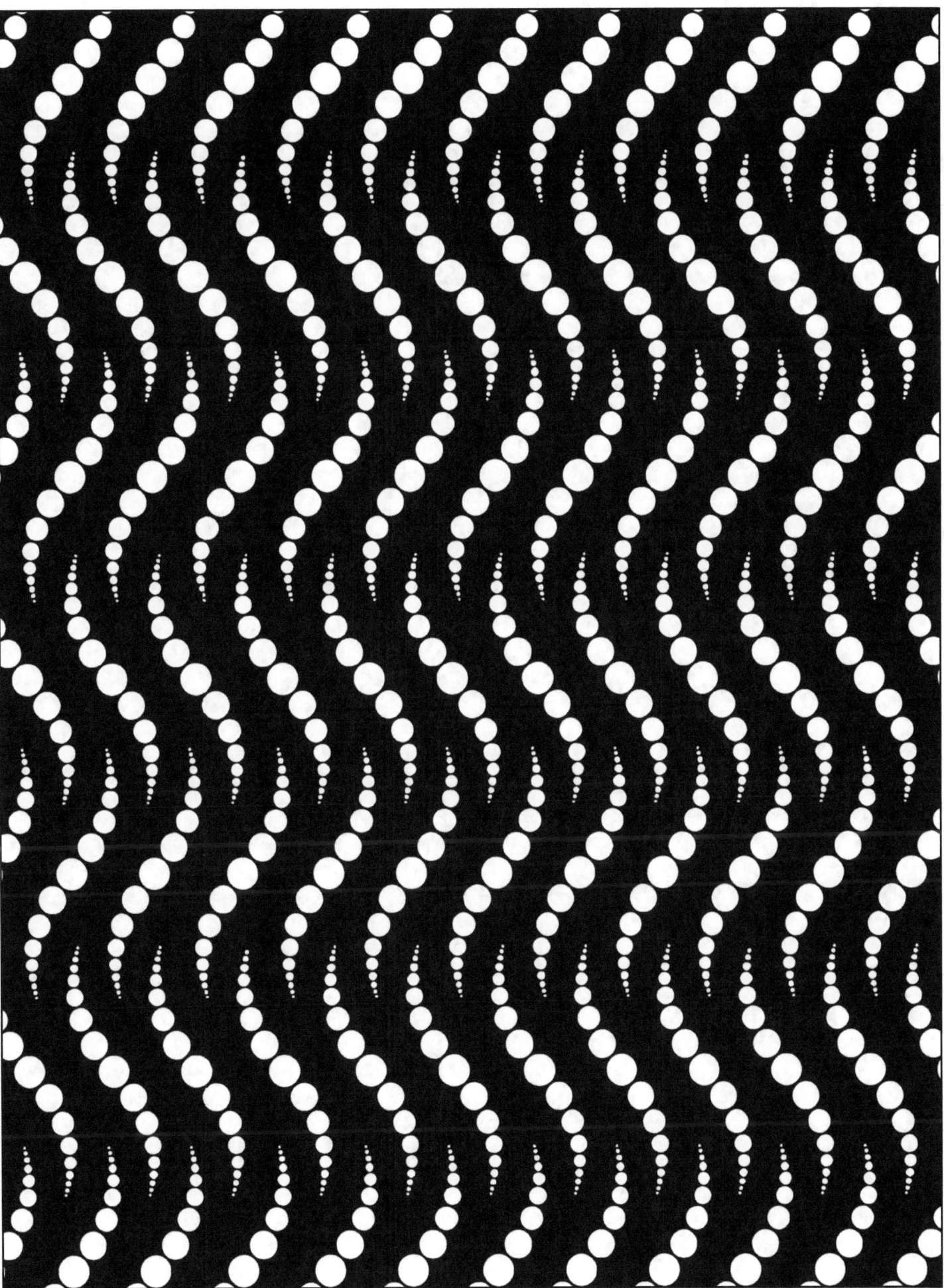

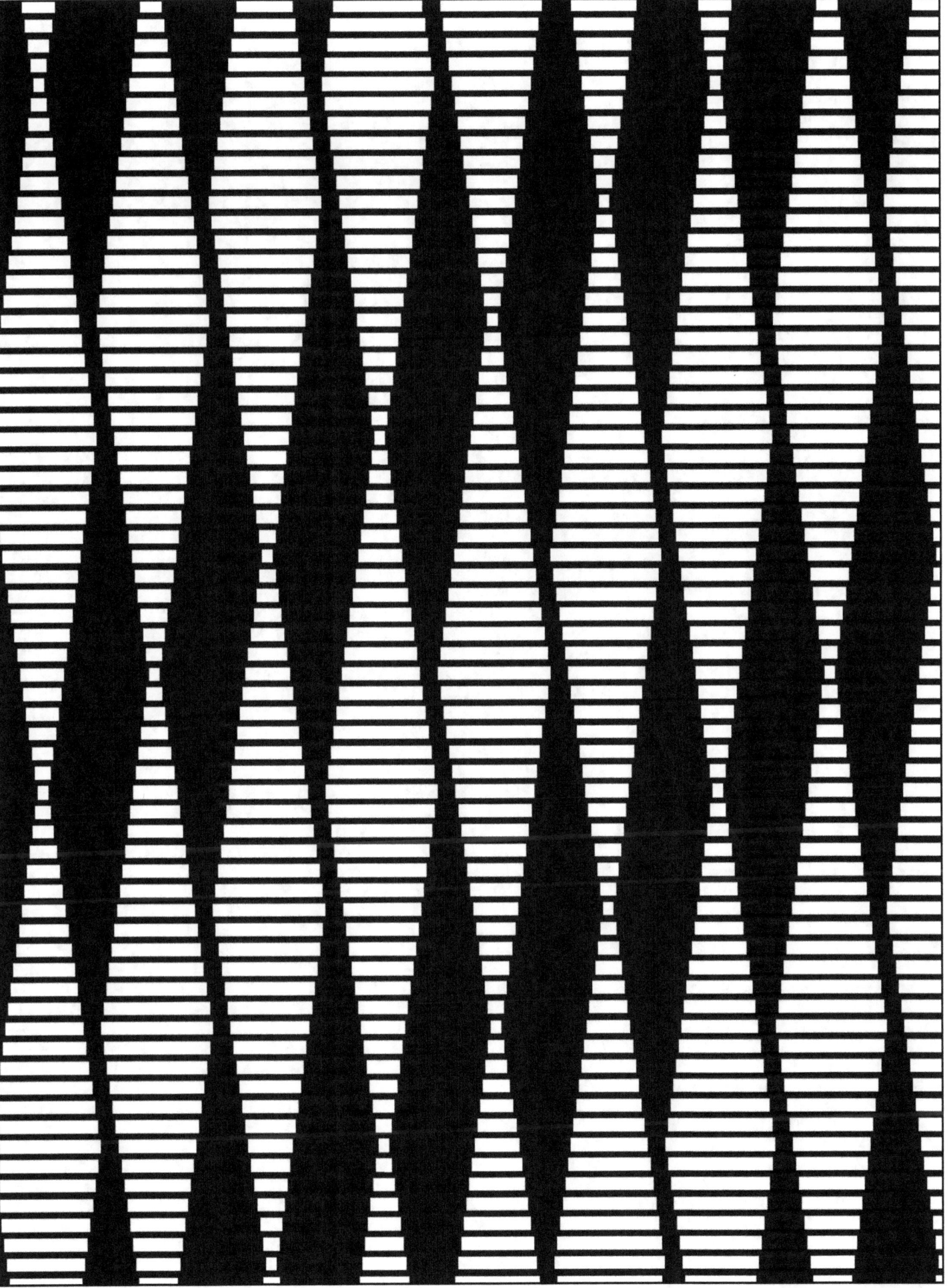

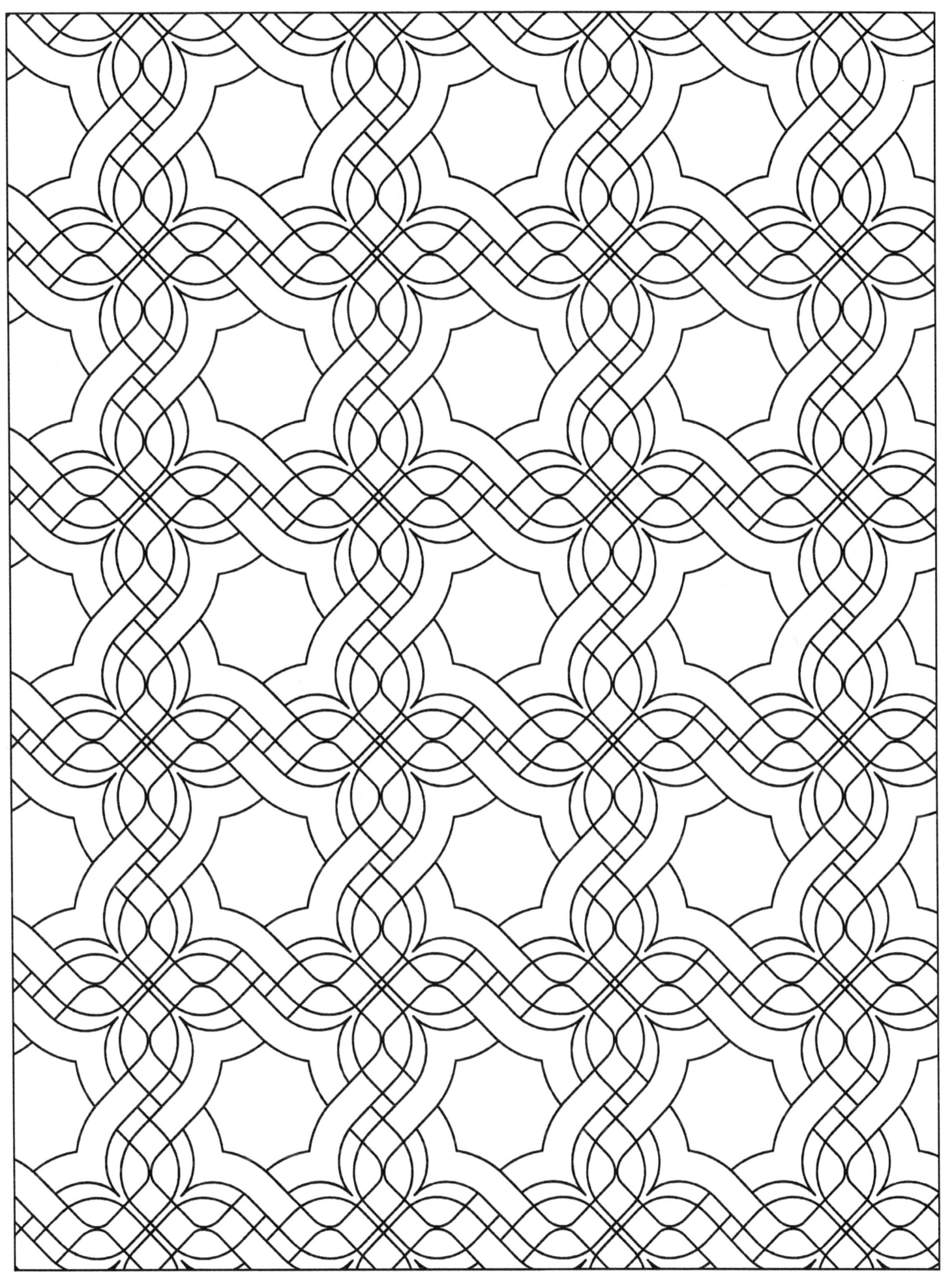

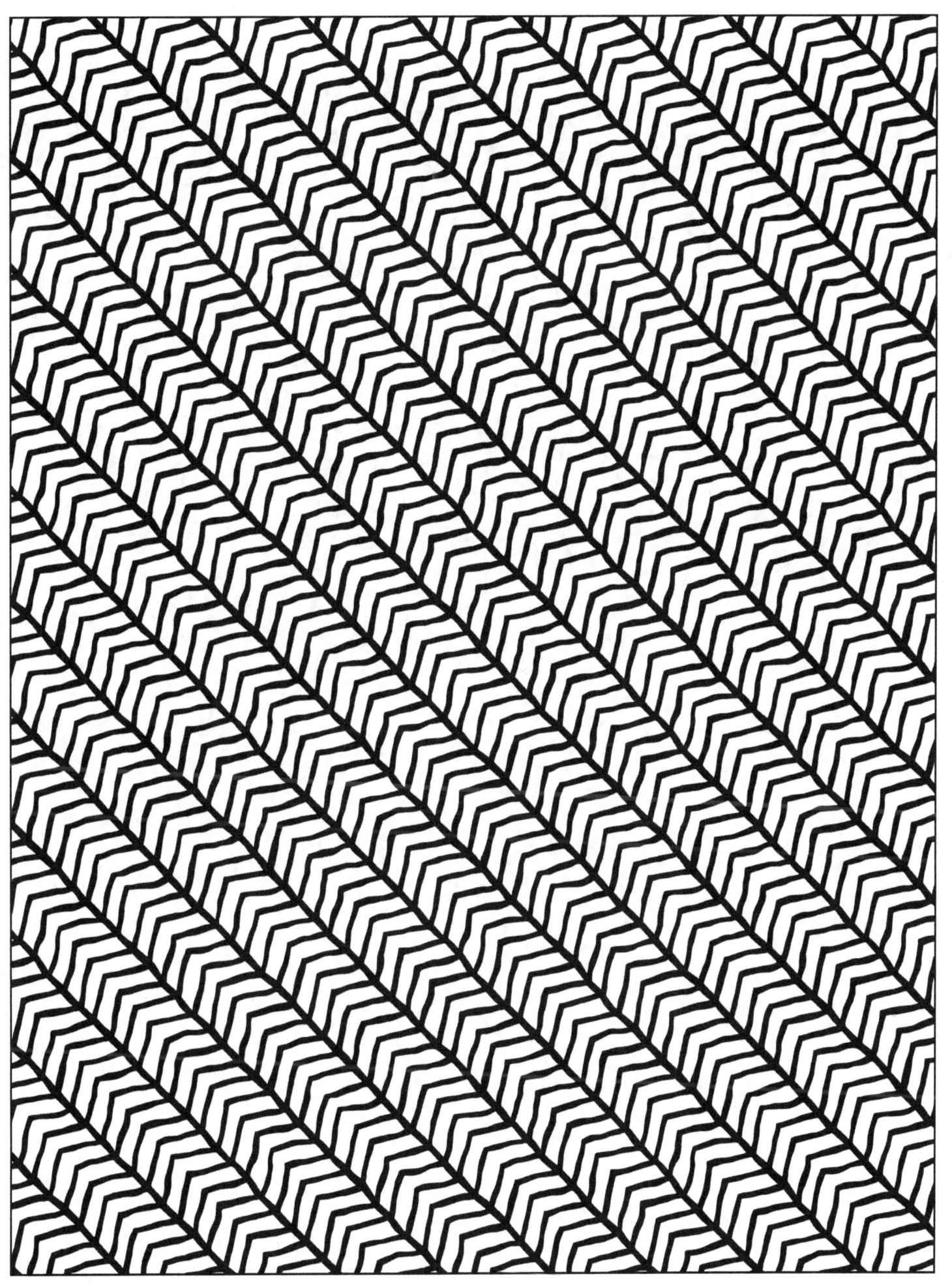

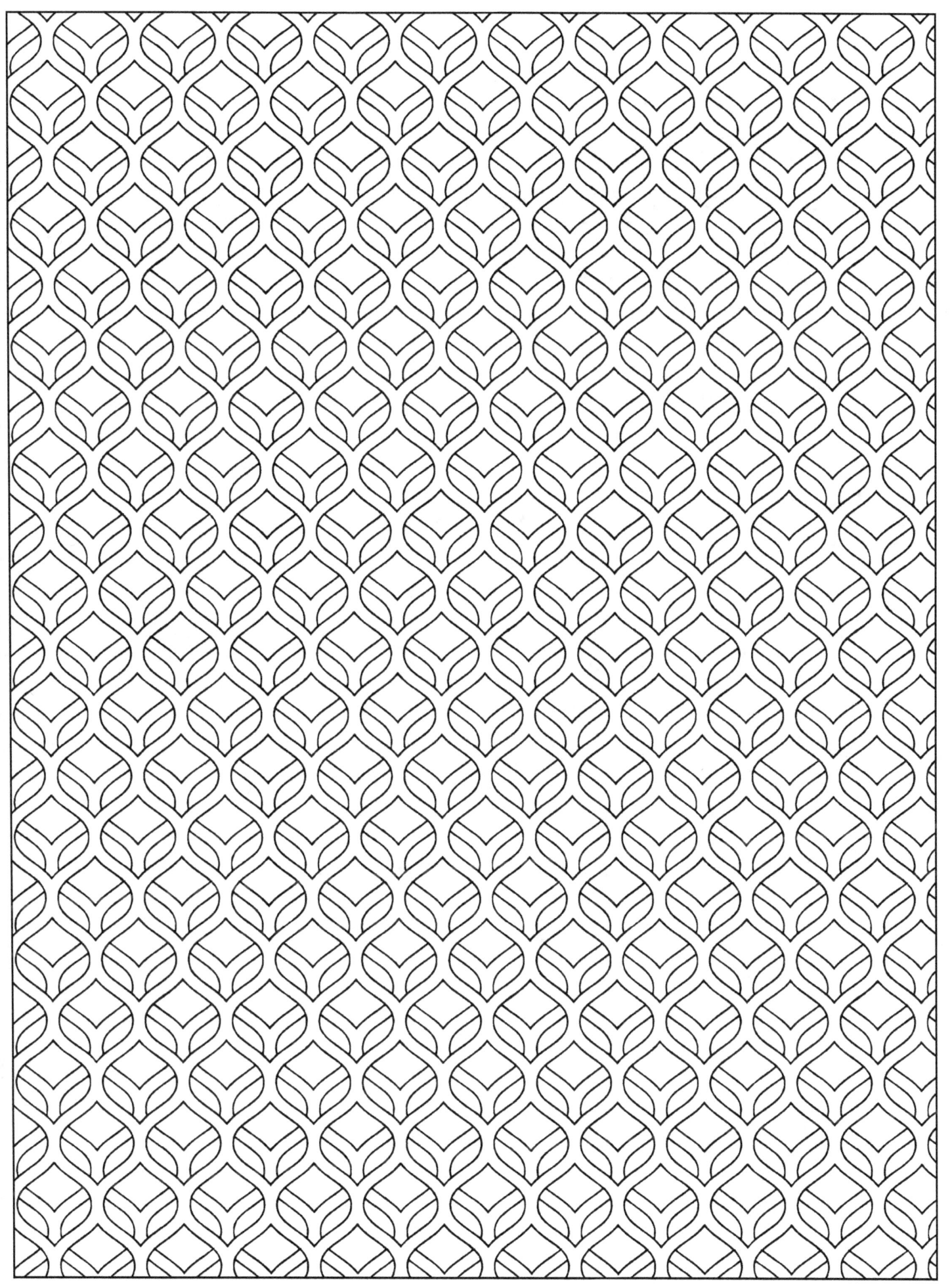

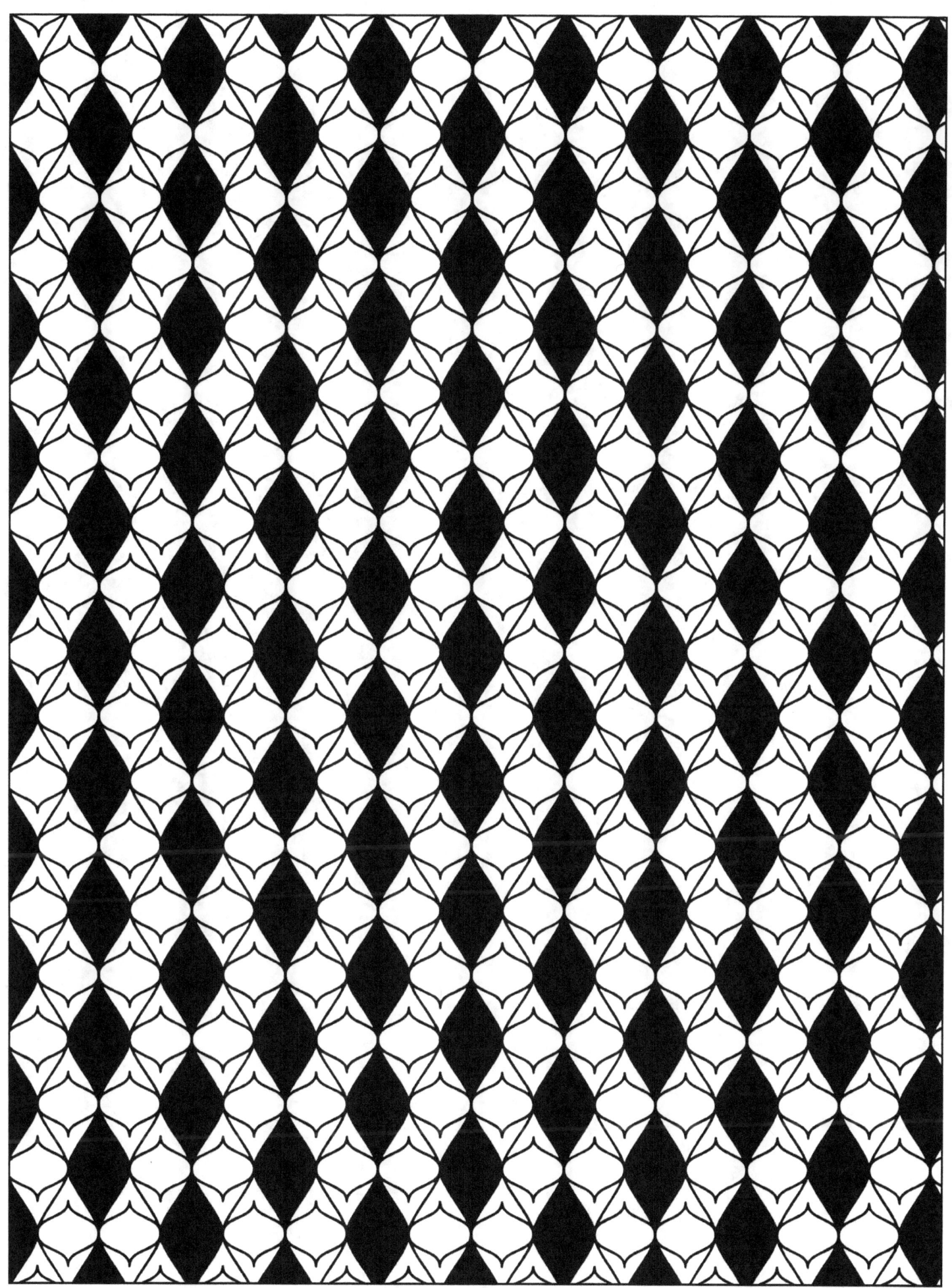

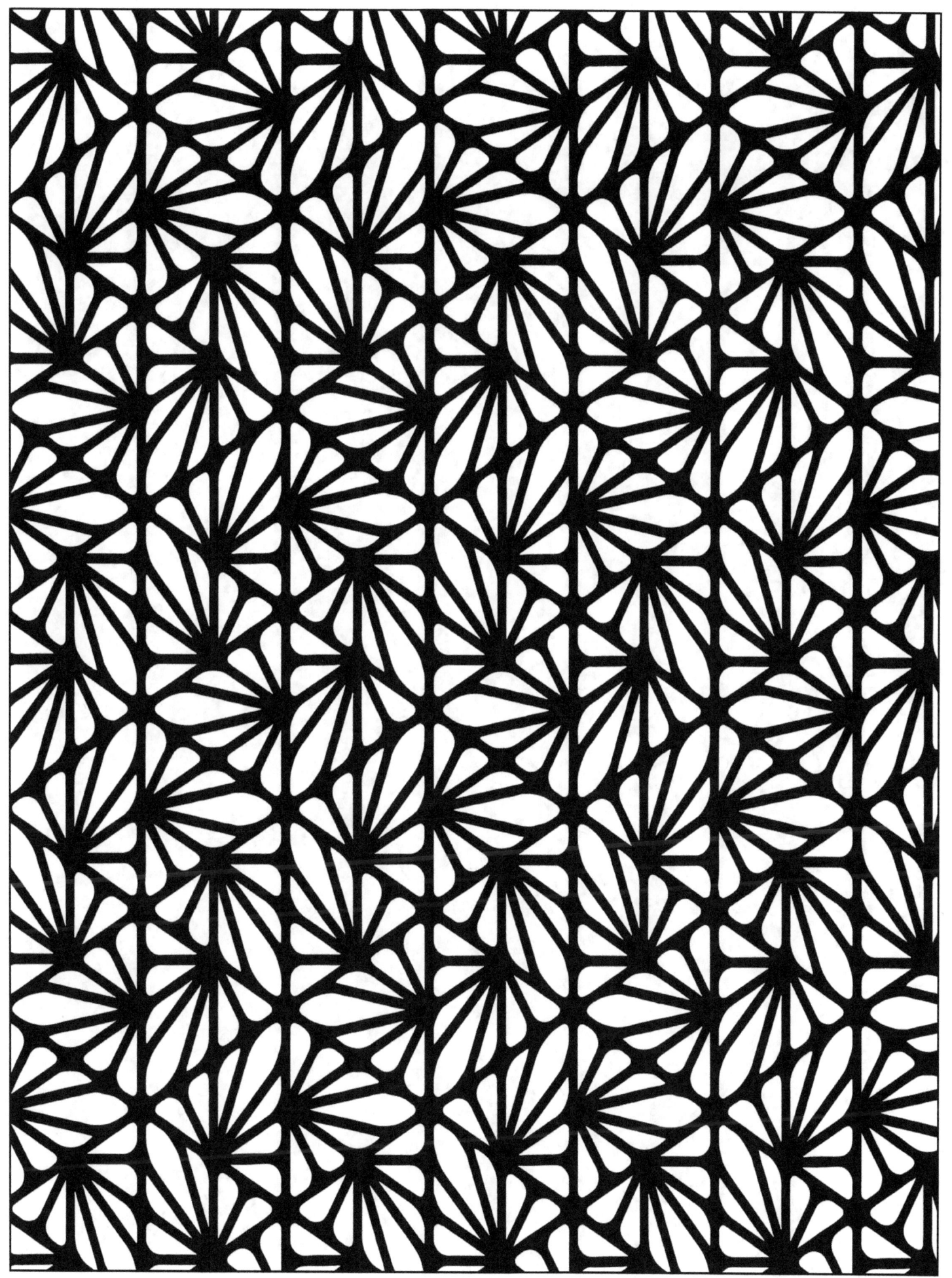

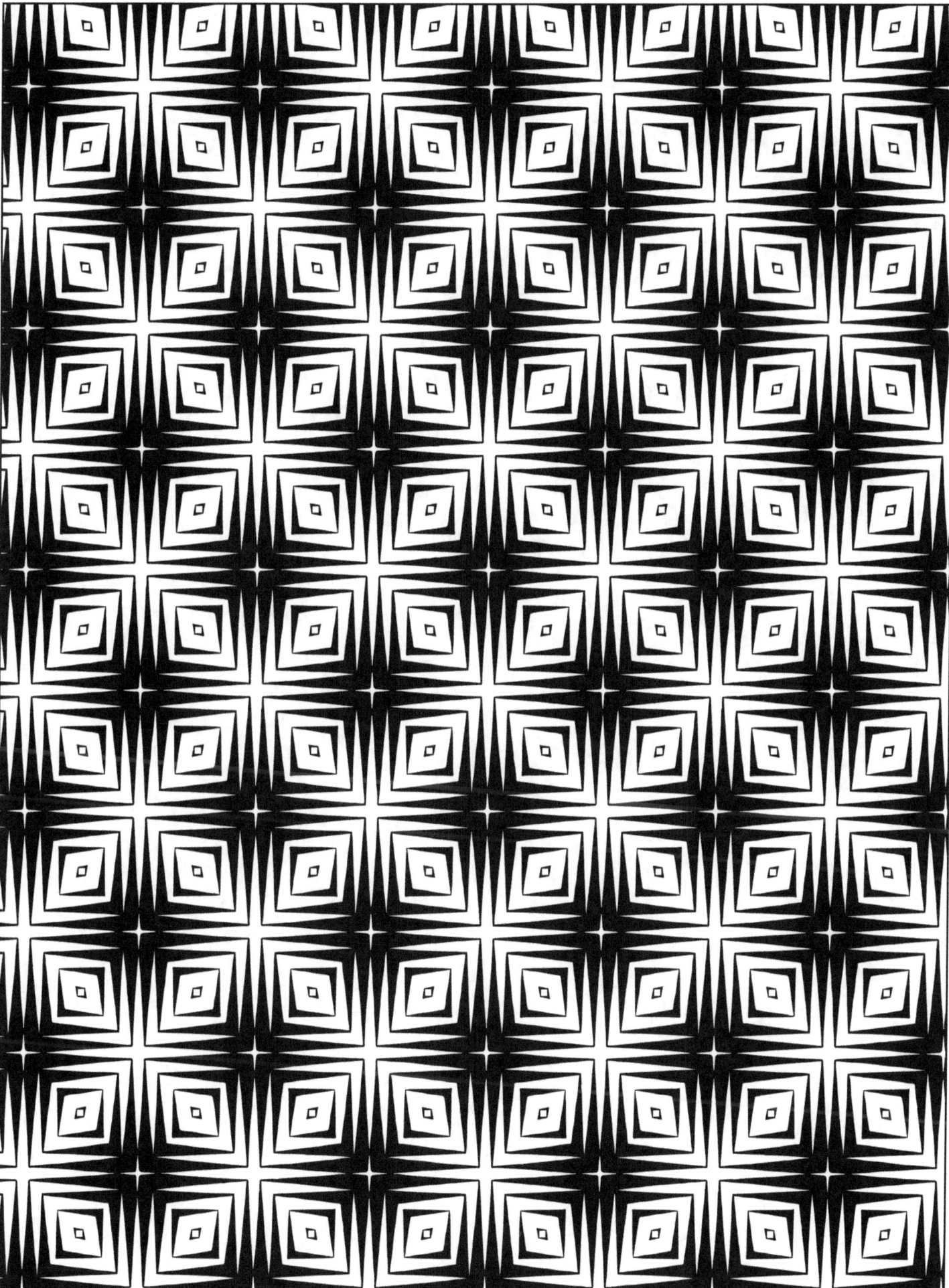

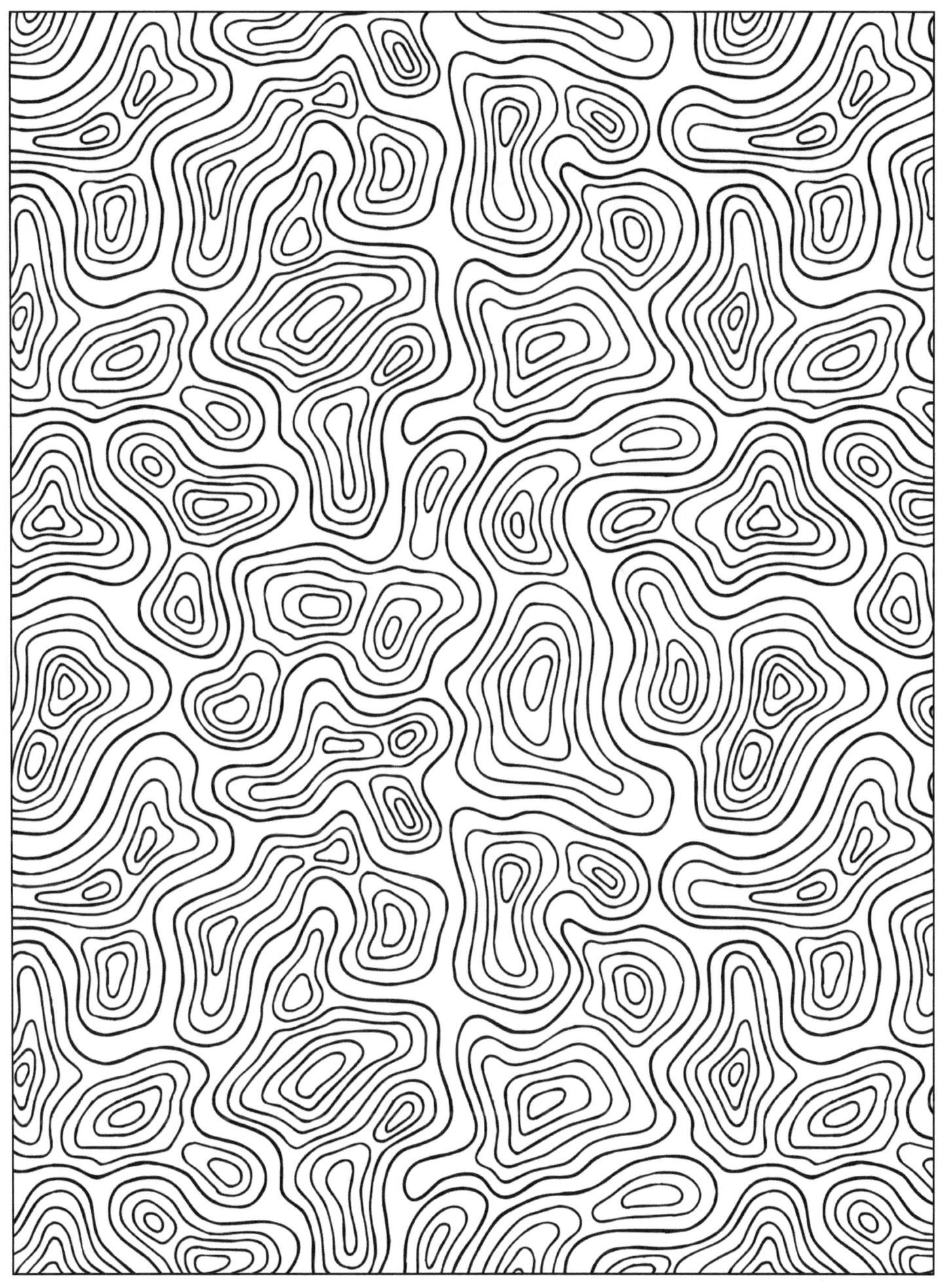

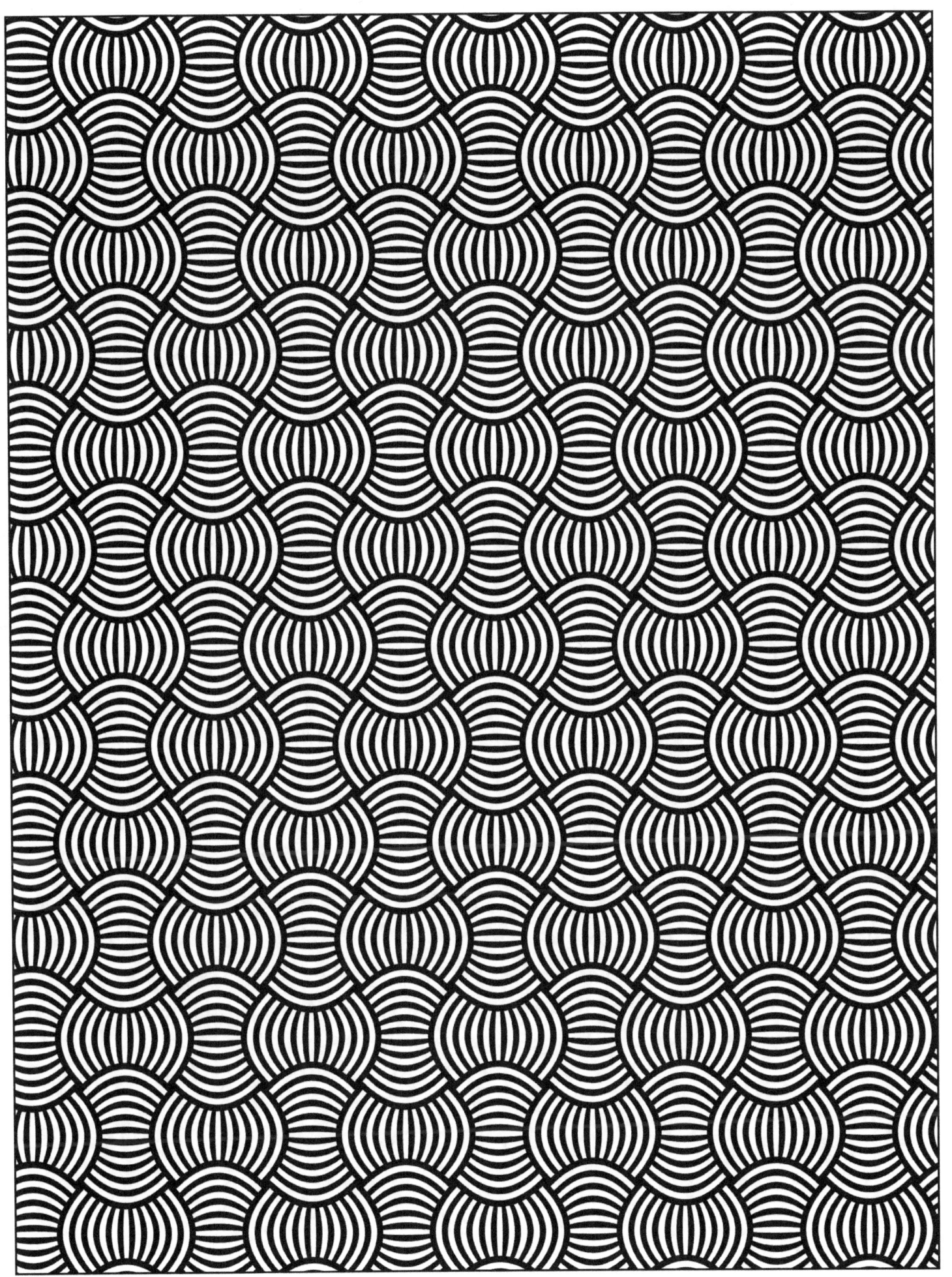

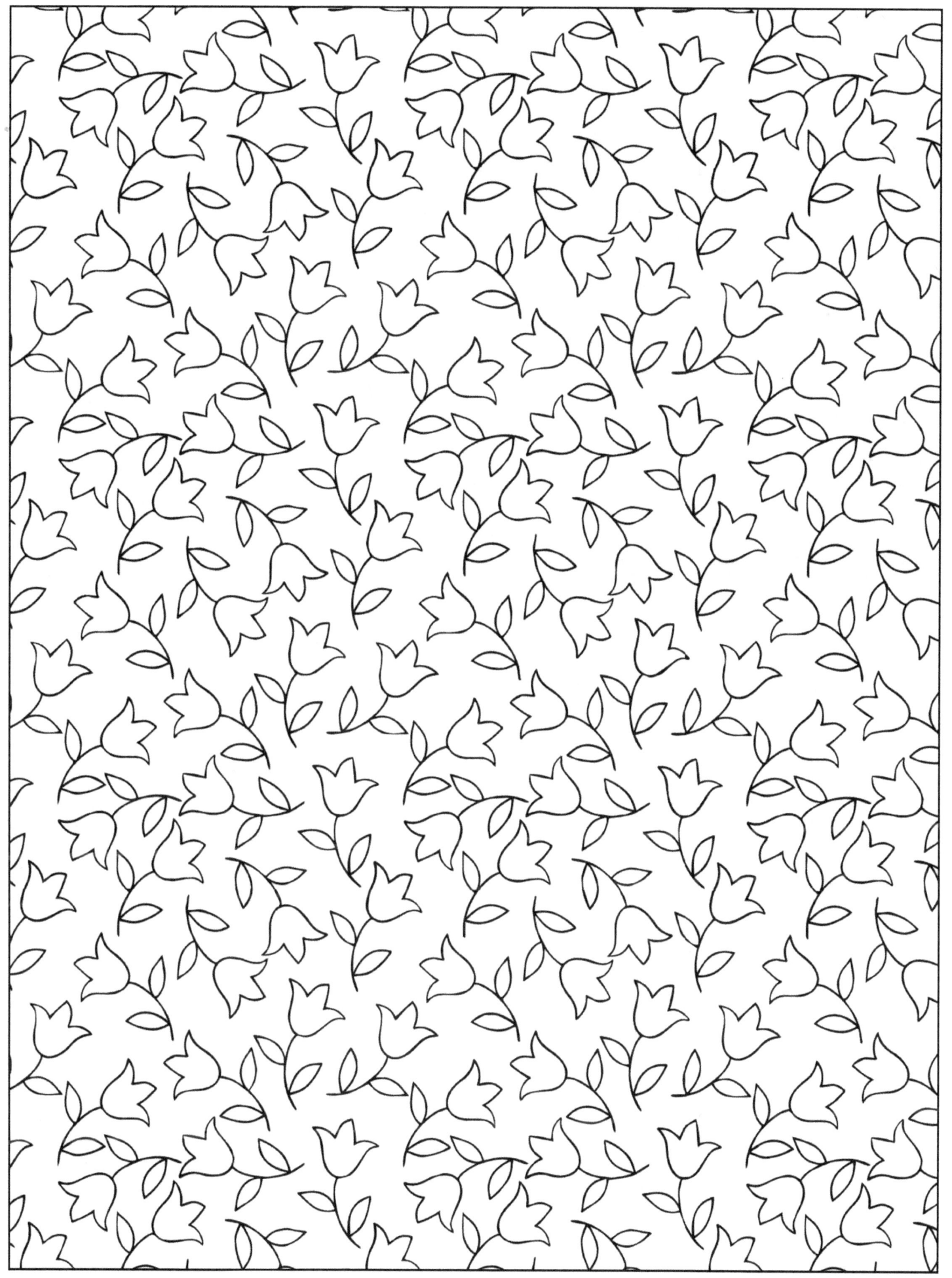

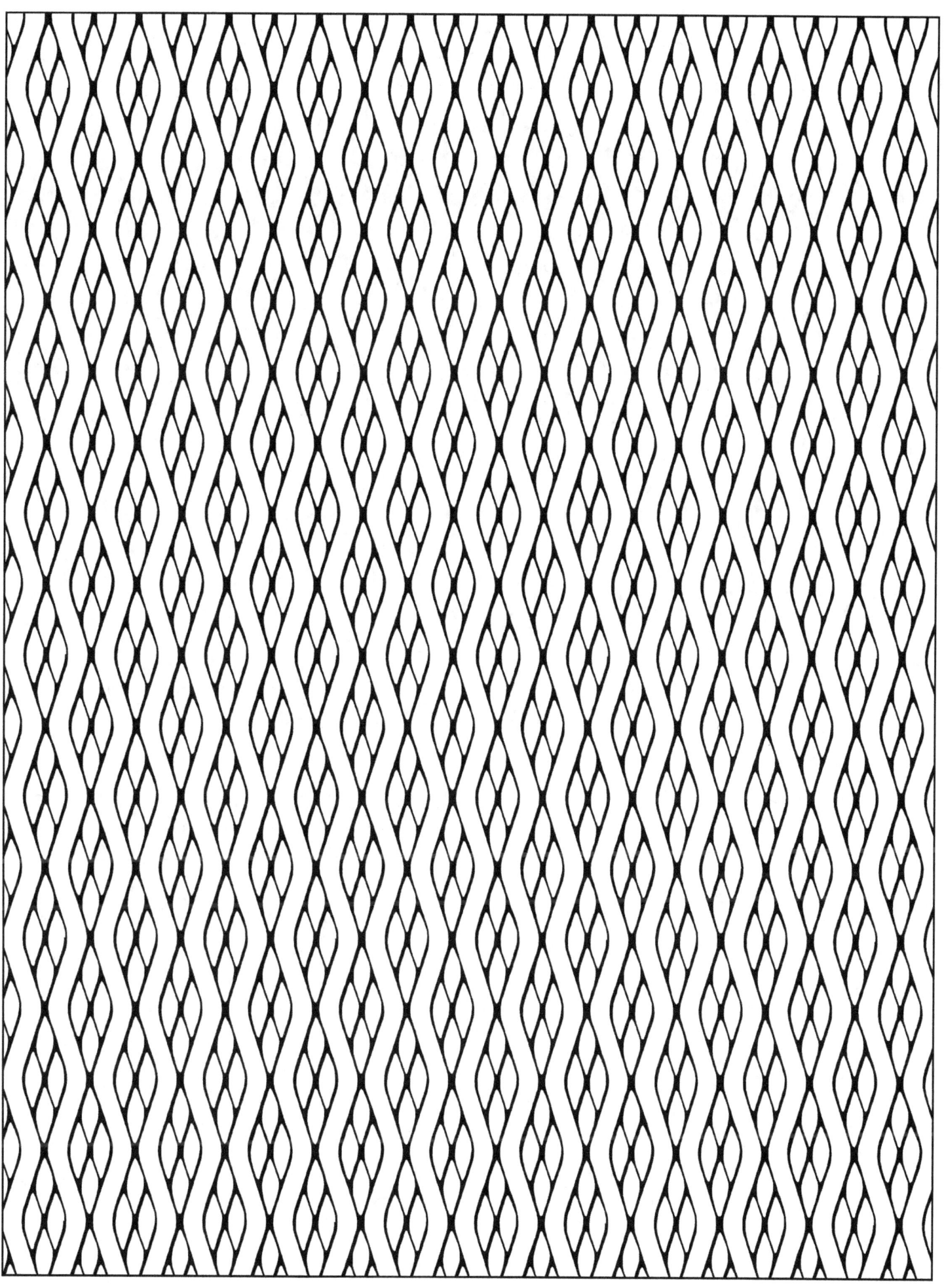

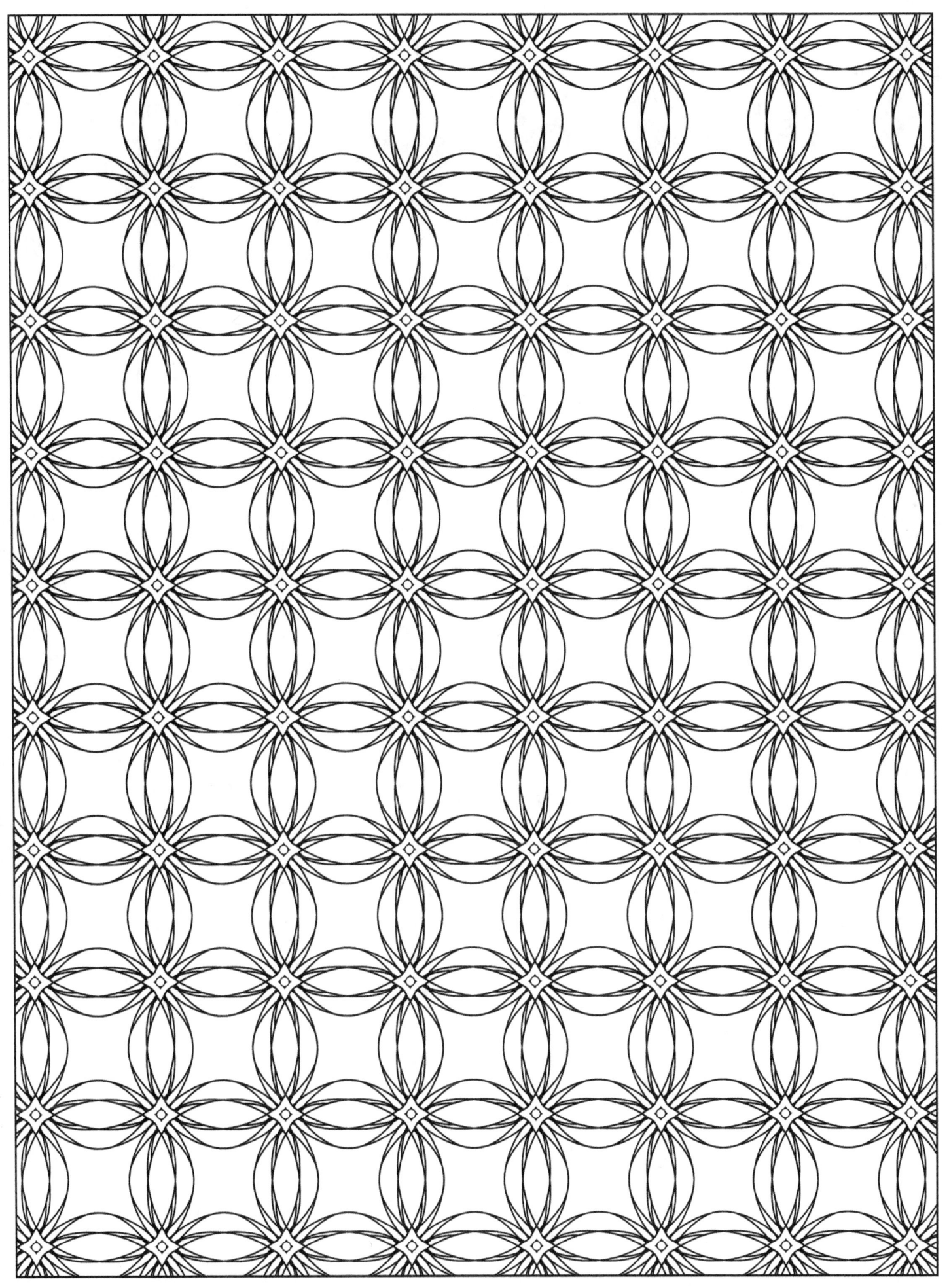

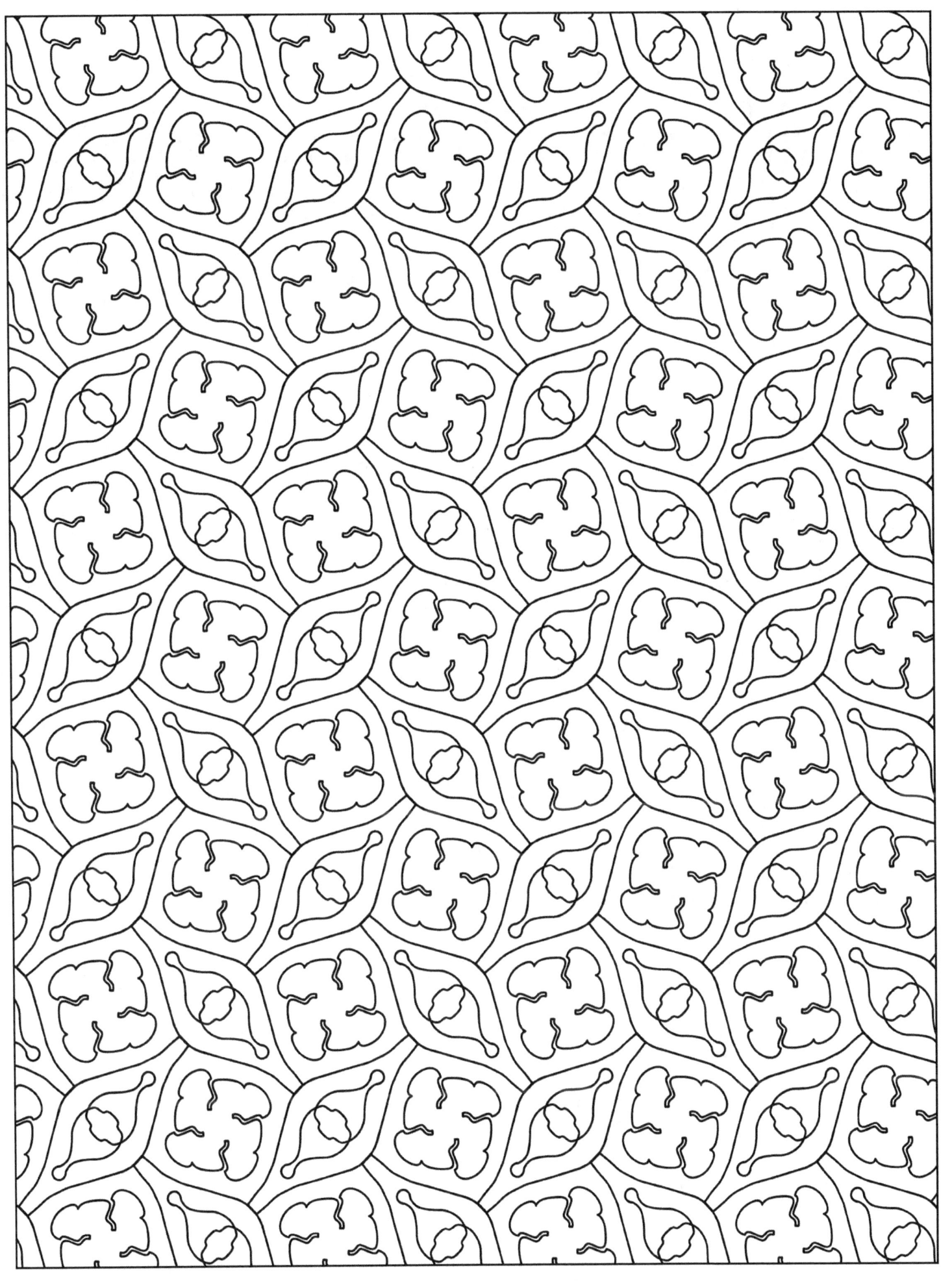

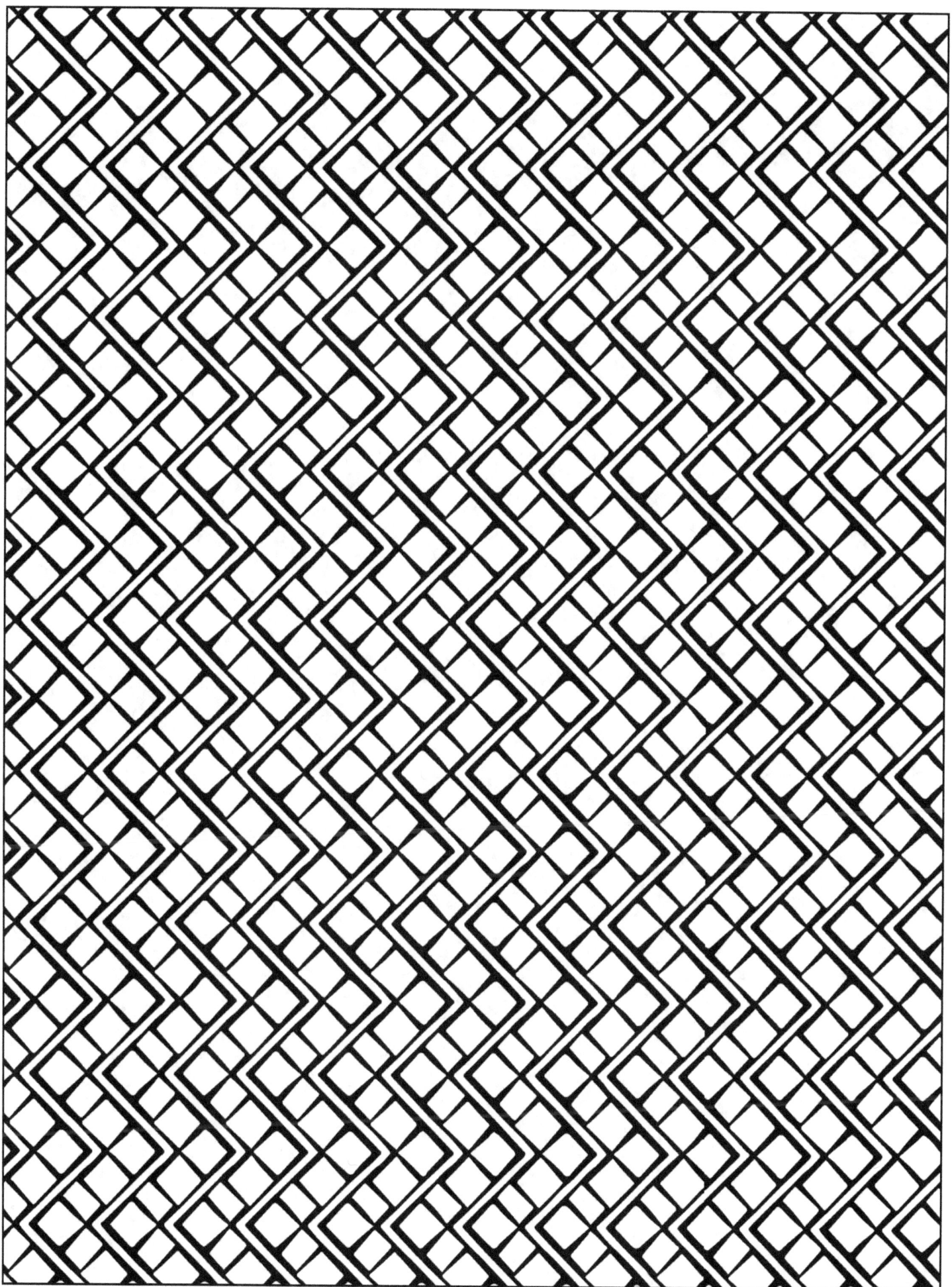

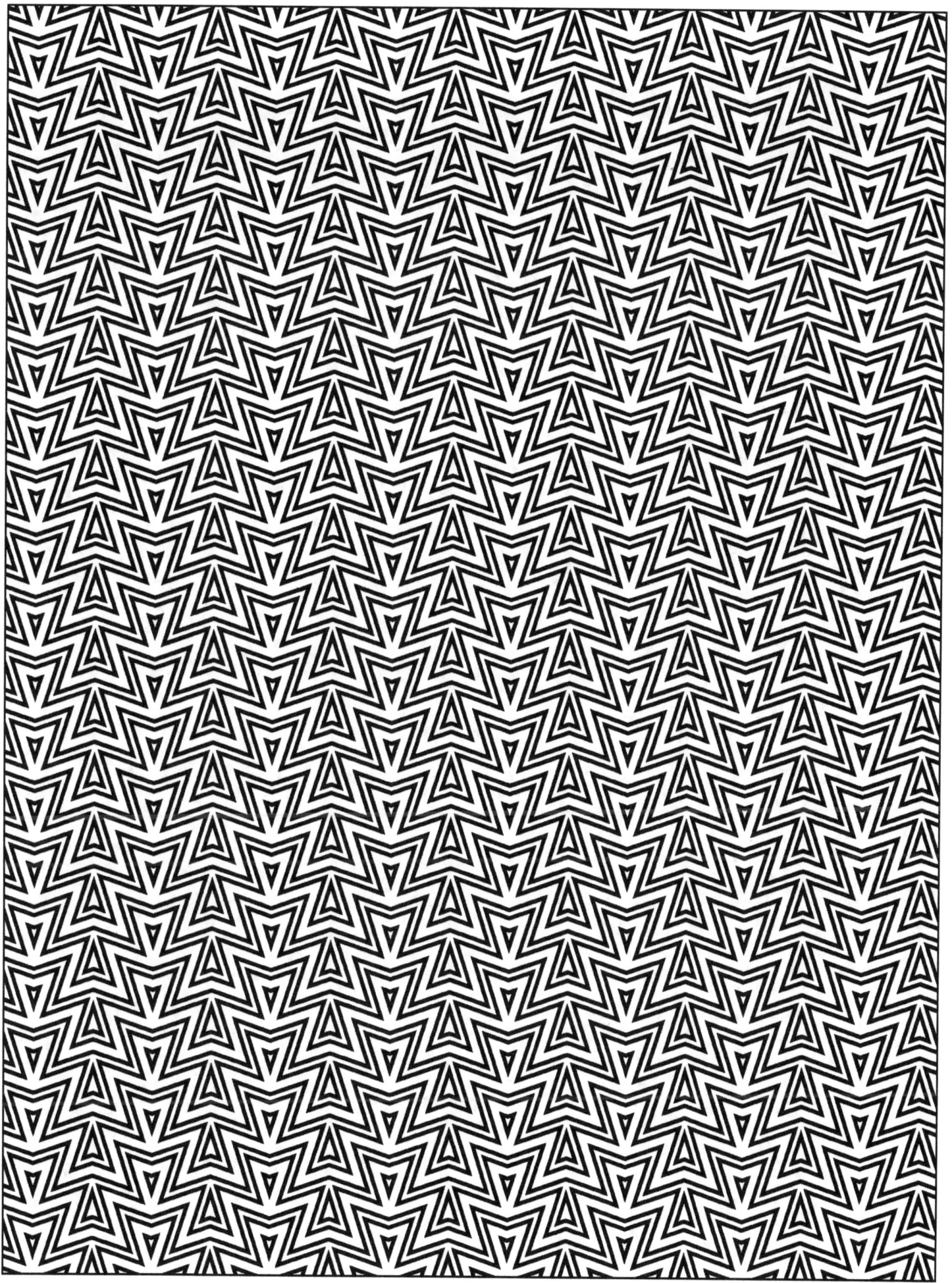

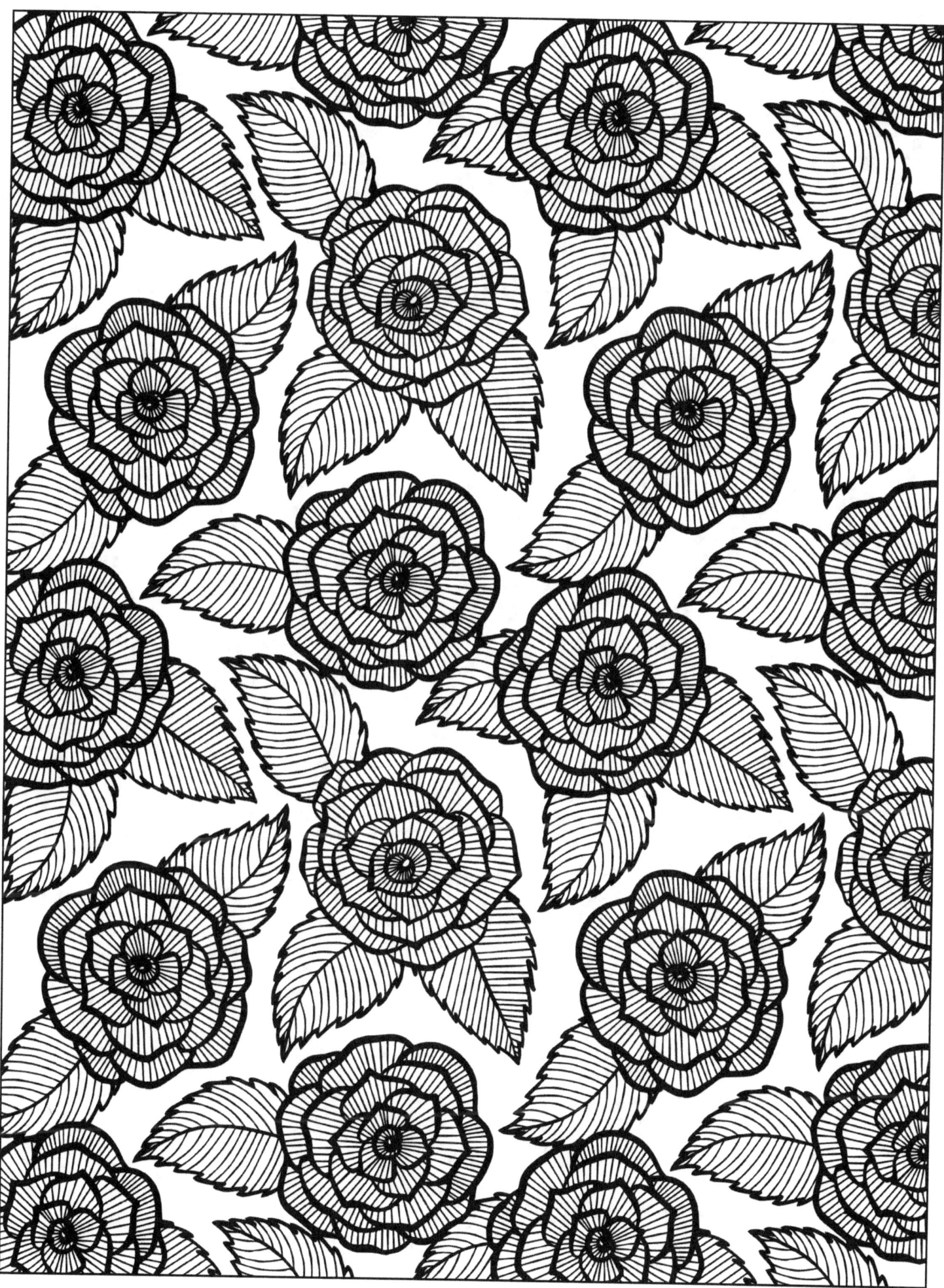

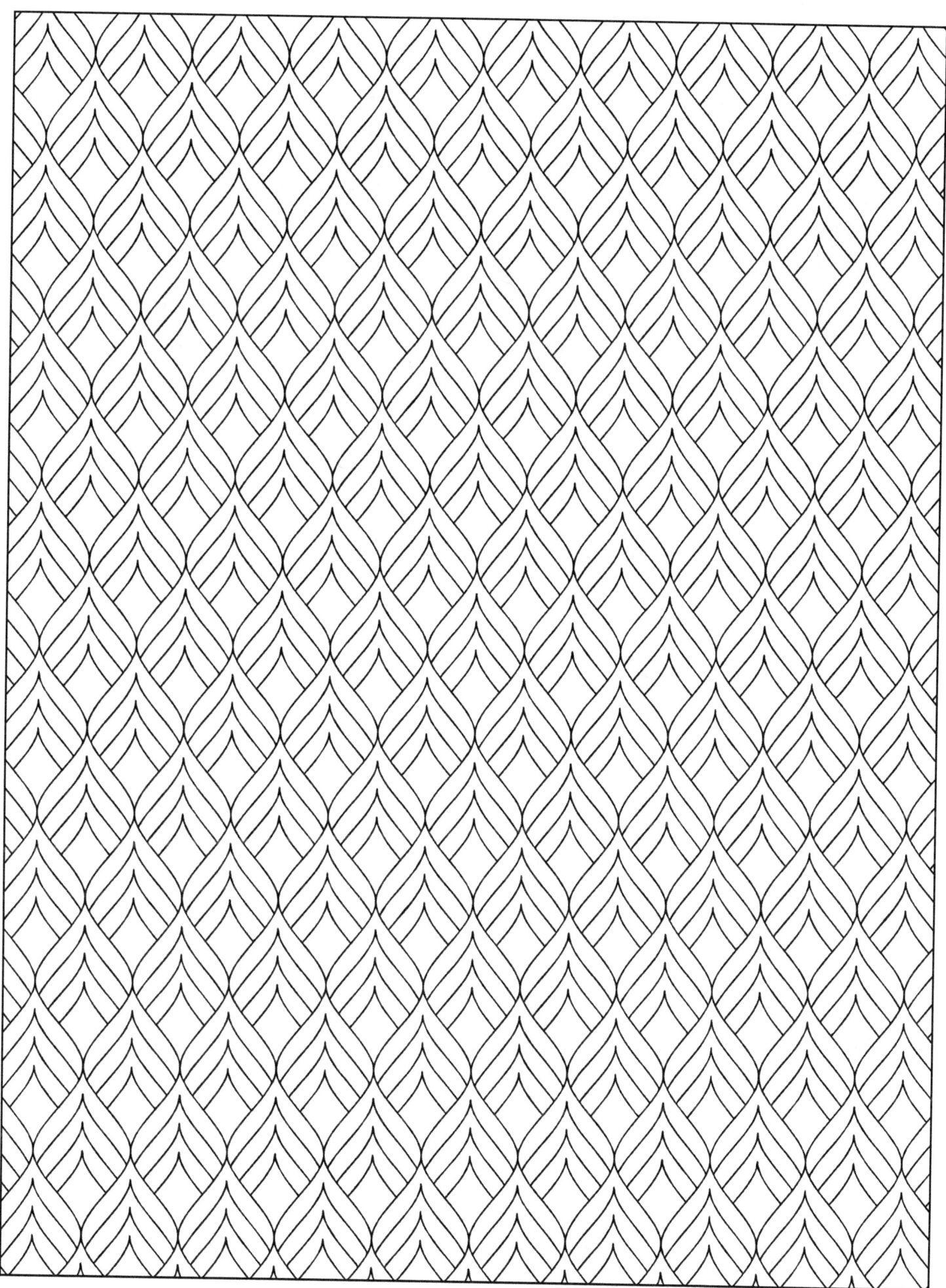

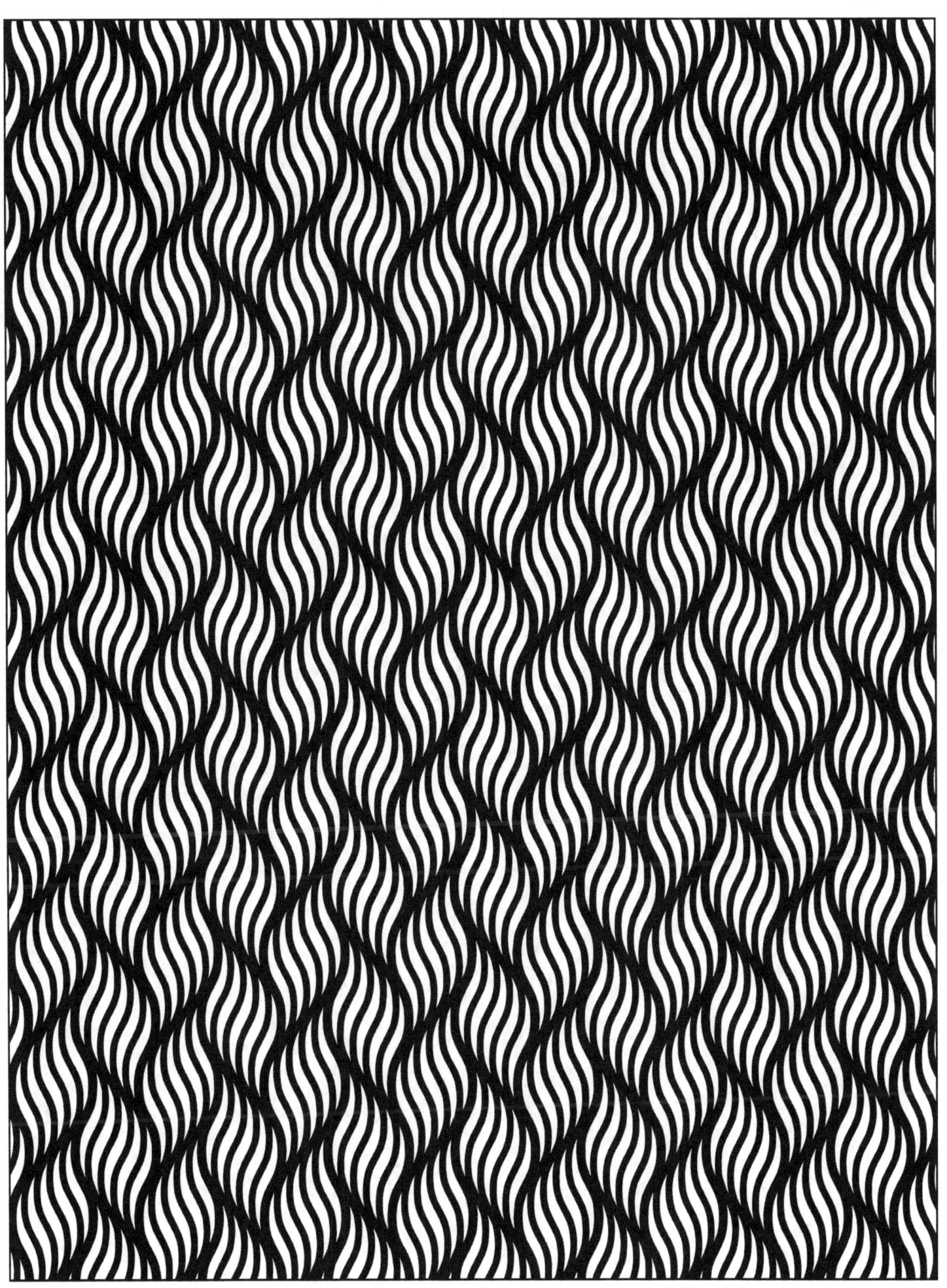

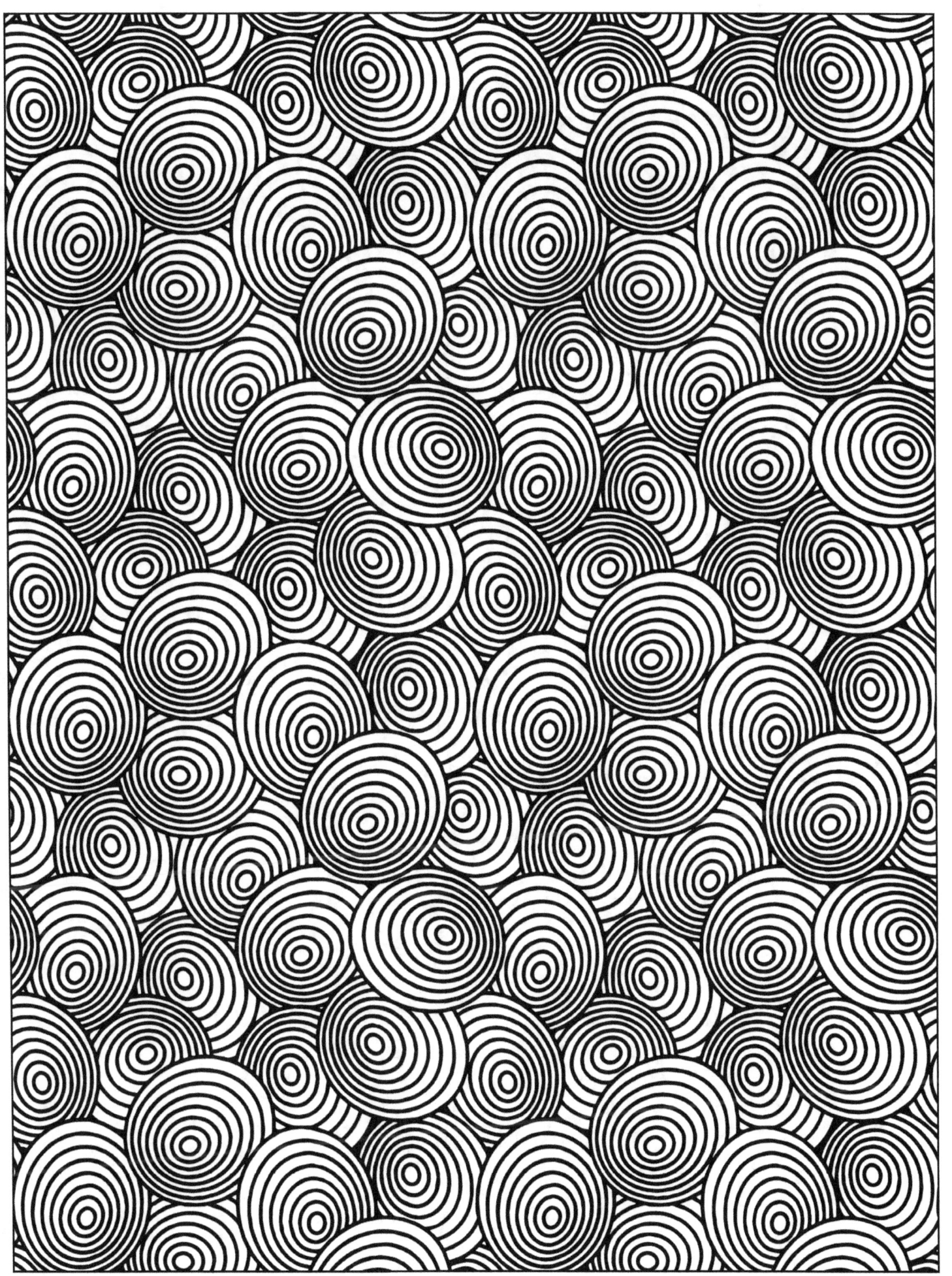

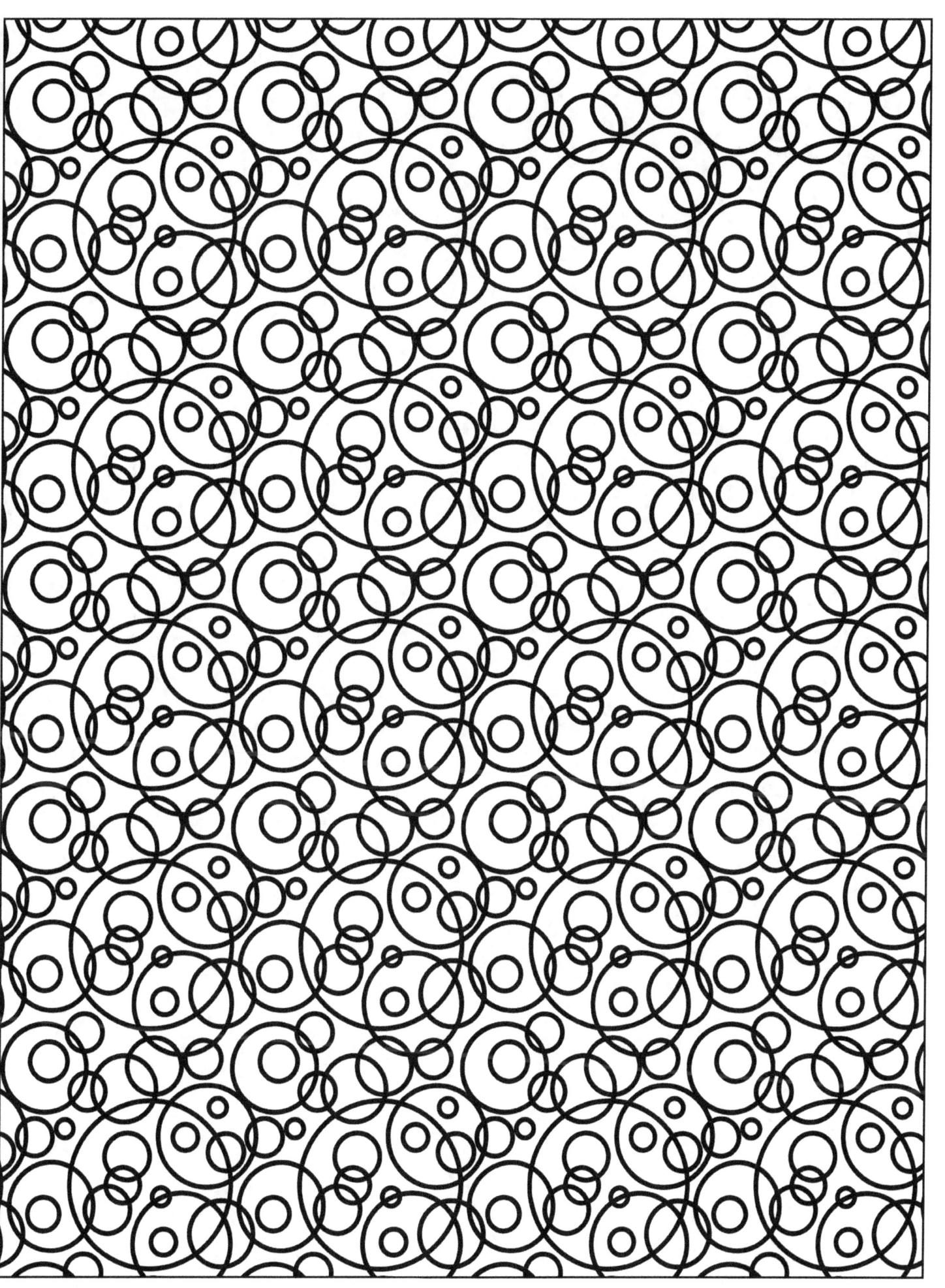

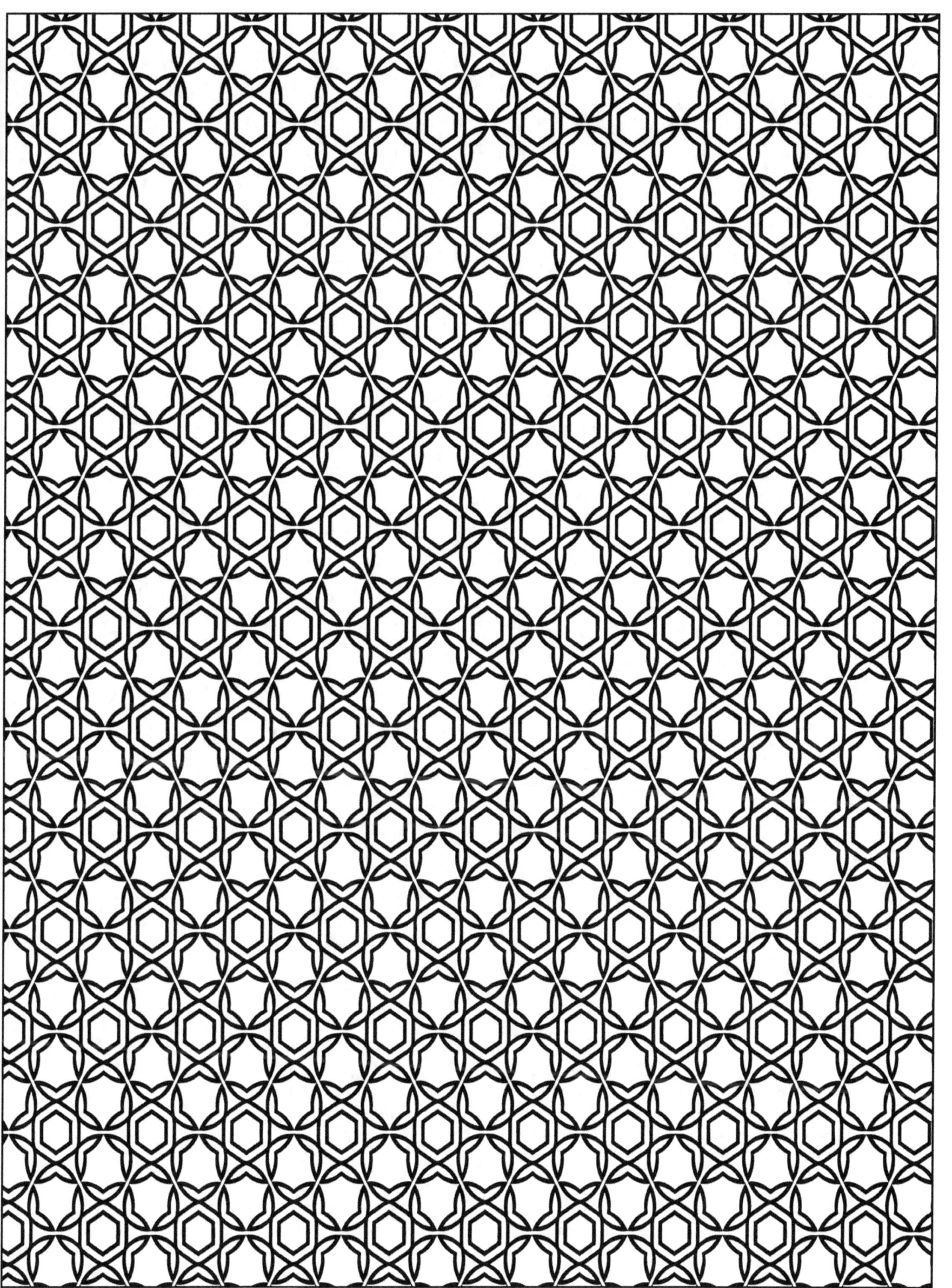

www.ingramcontent.com/pod-product-compliance
Lightning Source LLC
Chambersburg PA
CBHW062222220526
45471CB00009B/3305